Agamben's Joyful Kafka

Agamben's Joyful Kafka

Finding Freedom Beyond Subordination

Anke Snoek

BLOOMSBURY
NEW DELHI • LONDON • OXFORD • NEW YORK • SYDNEY

BLOOMSBURY INDIA
Bloomsbury Publishing India Pvt. Ltd
Second Floor, Building No. 4
DDA Complex LSC, Pocket C – 6 & 7
Vasant Kunj, New Delhi 110070
www.bloomsbury.com

BLOOMSBURY, Bloomsbury Academic India and the Diana logo are trademarks of Bloomsbury Publishing Plc

First published in India 2019
First published 2012

This edition published with permission from Bloomsbury Publishing Plc, 50 Bedford Square, London, WC1B3DP, UK

British Library Cataloguing-in-Publication Data
A catalogue record for this book is available from the British Library.

Library of Congress Cataloging-in-Publication Data
A catalog record for this book is available from the Library of Congress

ISBN: 978-93-88912-17-4

2 4 6 8 10 9 7 5 3 1

Typeset by Fakenham Prepress Solutions, Fakenham, Norfolk NR21 8NN
Printed and bound in India by Replika Press Pvt. Ltd.

For Joep Dohmen

It is a very poor reading of Kafka's works that sees in them only a summation of the anguish of a guilty man before the inscrutable power.

Giorgio Agamben

Contents

Acknowledgements

I feel lucky to have a friend like Ruud van der Helm. The idea for this book originated on the veranda of his house in Accra. His intelligence, power, creativity and honesty helped me through many challenging moments. This book would not have existed without his help. Secondly my thanks go to my editor, Haaris Naqvi, for his help in publishing this book.

Marije Nieuwenhuis was the first reader of the manuscript and her lucid comments and cheerful suggestions were of great help for me. I also owe many thanks to Jaap Gruppelaar, Cas Barendregt, Colby Dickinson, Robert Sinnerbrink and Nitzan Lebovic who gave me many useful comments on the different drafts of the text. Fabio Bazzoli and Kazumi Takakuwa helped me track down Italian, non-translated works by Agamben: thanks very much for this! Henry Jansen, Esther Schwemmlein, Susanna Petruccelli, Emily Margo and Jeffrey Bussolini helped with different translations. Cerise Howard edited the final draft for me, many thanks for that.

There are a number of people who contributed to my study of Agamben in the last few years. Leon Heuts of *Filosofie Magazine* first introduced me to Agamben's work. Gijsbert van der Heijden, Toshiro Osawa, Aydin Pourmoslemi and Laurens Ten Kate not only took part in many discussions with me about Agamben, but also became my friends. The book shop "de Rooie Rat" in Utrecht and Joop Maassen always had the right books in stock when I needed them.

Finally, I want to thank my family and friends for their support: my parents Bert and Annelies; my sisters Gerda and Harriëtte; Josje and my friend Kim Koopman. Finally I want to thank my partner, Caspar van Genuchten, for his unconditional support and love.

Abbreviations

CC *The Coming Community, Notes on politics*. Minneapolis: University of Minnesota Press, 1993.

ELJ Agamben, Giorgio and Judith Butler. *Eichmann, Law and Justice*: http://www.egs.edu/faculty/giorgio-agamben/videos/eichmann-law-and-justice/, 2009.

EP *The End of the Poem: Studies in Poetics*. Stanford, California: Stanford University Press, 1999.

ER 'The Eternal Return and the Paradox of Passion.' *Stanford Italian Review* 6, no. 1–2 (1986): 9–17.

HS *Homo Sacer: Sovereign Power and Bare Life*. Stanford, CA: Stanford University Press, 1998.

IH *Infancy and History: The Destruction of Experience*. London; New York: Verso, 1993.

IM *Image et Mémoire. Écrits Sur L'image, La Danse et Le Cinéma*. Paris: Desclée de Brouwer, 2004.

IP *Idea of Prose*. Albany: State University of New York Press, 1995.

K 'K'. In *The Work of Giorgio Agamben: Law, Literature, Life*, edited by Nicholas Heron, Justin Clemens and Alex Murray, 66–81. Edinburgh: Edinburgh University Press, 2008.

KG *The Kingdom and the Glory: For a Theological Genealogy of Economy and Government. Homo Sacer Ii.2.* Stanford, CA: Stanford University Press, 2011.

LD *Language and Death: The Place of Negativity*. Minneapolis: University of Minnesota Press, 1991.

MS 'The Messiah and the Sovereign: The Problem of Law in Walter Benjamin'. In *Potentialities: Collected Essays in Philosophy*, edited by W. Hamacher & D. E. Wellbery, 160–77. Stanford, CA: Stanford University Press, 1999/1992.

MWC *The Man without Content*. Stanford, CA: Stanford University Press, 1999.

MWE *Means without End: Notes on Politics, Theory out of Bounds*. Minneapolis: University of Minnesota Press, 2000.

N *Nudities*. Stanford, CA: Stanford University Press, 2010.

O *The Open: Man and Animal*. Stanford, CA: Stanford University Press, 2004.

OT 'On Tiqqun'. http://anarchistwithoutcontent.wordpress.com/2010/04/18/tiqqun-apocrypha-repost, 2009.

P *Profanations*. New York: Zone Books, 2007.

PB 'Il Pozzo Di Babele'. *Tempo presente* 11, no. November (1966): 42–50.

PO *Potentialities: Collected Essays in Philosophy*, Meridian: Crossing Aesthetics. Stanford, CA: Stanford University Press, 1999.

QGK 'Quattro Glosse a Kafka'. *Rivista di estetica* 26, no. 22 (1986): 37–44.

RA *Remnants of Auschwitz: The Witness and the Archive*. New York: Zone Books, 1999.

RW 'Warum War Und Ist Robert Walser So Wichtig?' Lecture in *Akademie der Künste*, Berlin, 2005.

S *Stanzas: Word and Phantasm in Western Culture, Theory and History of Literature*. Minneapolis: University of Minnesota Press, 1993.

SE *State of Exception*. Chicago: University of Chicago Press, 2005.

ST *The Signature of All Things: On Method*. New York: Zone Books, 2009.

TI 'The Thing Itself'. *Contemporary Italian Thought* 16.2, no. 53 (1987): 18–28.

TL 'The Time That Is Left'. *Epoché* 7, no. 1 (2002): 1–14.

TR *The Time That Remains: A Commentary on the Letter to the Romans*. Stanford, CA: Stanford University Press, 2005.

VBH 'Vorwort'. In *Die Beamten Des Himmels: Über Engel*, 11–27. Frankfurt am Main/Leipzig: Verlag der Weltreligionen, 2007.

WA *'What Is an Apparatus?' And Other Essays*. Stanford, CA: Stanford University Press, 2009.

WM 'The Work of Man'. In *Giorgio Agamben: Sovereignty and Life*, edited by Matthew Calarco and Steven DeCaroli, 1–11. Stanford, CA: Stanford University Press, 2007.

WP 'What Is a Paradigm?' http://www.egs.edu/faculty/agamben/agamben-what-is-a-paradigm-2002.html, 2002.

Introduction: Kafka's Hope

People who use the word 'Kafkaesque' have probably never read Kafka.
(Stanley Kubrick)[1]

Franz Kafka and Giorgio Agamben. The endless fascination with Kafka's prose and the growing interest in Agamben's controversial philosophy are deeply rooted in their seemingly gloomy political world views. For both, the democratic, constitutional nation-state that claims transparency and security with its orderly procedures and universal laws is essentially grounded in the might of bureaucratic, administrative and legal violence. *The Trial*, arguably Kafka's most disconcerting story, heralded this invisible threat in a very lucid way, long before the Nazi concentration camps would take it to its horrifying, though logical, end.

Despite the many analyses and rereadings of Kafka's work, it remains difficult to capture its full political significance. Giorgio Agamben, one of the most important thinkers of our current time, transposes a number of Kafka's intuitions into concrete contemporary examples and their legal roots. In a provocative way, he decorticates the democratic state that, with its constitutionally grounded good intentions, is delivering its citizens more and more into the hands of legal violence.

Agamben refers to Kafka regularly in his works. He usually does so very briefly – a sentence, a word – even though he also devoted several longer essays to Kafka. Some of these writings have not been translated from Italian yet. There is no doubt about the importance of Kafka for Agamben's work, but, surprisingly, this influence has not been analysed in a systemic way. To date, there has been no single comprehensive treatment of the importance of Kafka's work for Agamben, or of the insights Agamben's philosophy offers for new Kafka interpretations. The secondary literature on Agamben often mentions his affinity for Kafka, but discussions usually focus on his interpretation of 'Before the Law' and 'In the Penal Colony'. The secondary literature on Kafka is slowly beginning to pay attention to the insights on Kafka found in Agamben's work – particularly Dolar, Santner and Minden.[2] But, generally speaking, the secondary literature is limited to only one narrow point of

[1] Michael Herr, *Kubrick* (New York: Grove Press, 2001), 13.

[2] Mladen Dolar, *A Voice and Nothing More* (Cambridge: MIT Press, 2006); Michael Minden, 'Kafka's "Josephine Die Sängerin Oder Das Volk Der Mäuse"', *German Life and Letter* 62.3 (2009); Eric Santner, *On Creaturely Life: Rilke, Benjamin, Sebald* (Chicago and London: University of Chicago Press, 2006).

intersection, again revolving mainly around Agamben's interpretation of 'Before the Law'.

This book grew out of a comprehensive search for all of Agamben's references to Kafka aimed at understanding the latter's influence on the former. Unexpectedly, this also resulted in an unusual and most rewarding perspective on Kafka's legacy. Agamben uses Kafka not so much to support his dark political theories as to show a way out, an exit strategy from the present political situation. And, although at first glance, Agamben and Kafka appear to be groping blindly in their lack of consolation, it appears to be precisely the notion of a way out that connects them and that is so difficult, at times, to square with the darkness of their work. All who have read Kafka have been surprised by how funny his stories could be at certain points, even when the protagonist is exposed to unbearable oppression. The same can be said about Agamben's work: precisely when one least expects it, his philosophy suddenly provides a possibility, even though – as we will see throughout this book – these possibilities are subtle and could easily be overlooked: they tend to present themselves as a reversal, not as a revolution. As a cross-reading between these two authors, the purpose of this book is to show the various possibilities for reversing the catastrophic political situation in which we live. The lens of Agamben's interpretation of Kafka brings a theory of such possibilities to the fore.

Although much criticised for this, Agamben and Agamben's Kafka do not present us with a ready-to-use manual for a way out of our current political situation. Rather, that way out is to be formulated on the basis of an inversion that can be found in their work: a possibility or potential that lies enclosed within the current situation. The immanence of this possibility does not produce a universally applicable theory, a pattern that can be distinguished from or opposed to the law. In both Kafka and Agamben, the possibilities stand alone, as singularities. DeCauter once described Agamben's work as a contrast medium that allows us to see what was previously invisible. The cross-reading on which we are about to embark is intended to be a contrast medium as well, to alert us to power relations and to recognize the ways out of those relations.[3]

This introduction lays the foundation for the specific understanding of power and freedom found in Kafka and Agamben. The following chapters serve, first of all, to test the fruitfulness of Agamben's interpretation of Kafka. This interpretation will serve as the starting point and critical marginal notes and relevant discussions can be found in the footnotes. The

[3] Lieven DeCauter, 'De Bloedige Mystificaties Van De Nieuwe Wereldorde', *De witte raaf* 108 (2004), 7.

concluding chapter will bring together the rich yield that can be gathered from Agamben's interpretation of Kafka.

Kafka's legacy

Kafka's most famous book is, undoubtedly, *The Trial*. Without being aware that he has committed an offence, Joseph K. is arrested one morning in his bedroom. What follows is a tangle of murky procedures that seemingly inevitably end in his death, without his ever becoming aware of what the indictment or sentence was. It was this novella that led to the term 'Kafkaesque', a predicate that would constantly be associated with Kafka's work from then on. Like no other, Kafka describes how individuals are subjected to bureaucracy, with its laws and procedures. In *The Trial* – and, in fact, in all his works – an ominous threat can be sensed and this novella, like most of Kafka's other stories does not seem to turn out well. That our day-to-day life as citizens is more Kafkaesque than safe is considered to be the most prominent insight that Kafka has left us in his work.

The biographical view of Franz Kafka, the person that has developed out of this 'Kafkaesque message' emphasizes primarily his tragic side – not only in his work, but also in his life. This is the Kafka who became engaged several times and these engagements led to a fascinating exchange of letters but never to marriage.[4] This is the Kafka who lived with his parents until the age of 31, entangled in an interminable, hopeless conflict with his father. This is the Kafka who was not able to do anything but write and yet felt unable to write; who was constantly torn between his job at the insurance company and his ambitions as a writer; who suffered from a lack of recognition. This is the Kafka who, on his deathbed, asked his friend Max Brod to destroy his unpublished work. The famous photo of Kafka is often printed darker than it actually is and thus gives the impression of a shadow falling over his face.[5] According to many interpreters, this shadow falls over his work as well.

There is also another Kafka. Kafka was known for laughing exuberantly when his stories were read aloud at reading evenings with friends – and he was apparently the only one who did so. He had to laugh especially at those

[4] Jacqueline Raoul-Duval, *Kafka, L'éternel Fiancé* (Paris: Flammarion, 2011).

[5] As Dora Dymant describes: 'The essential characteristics of his face were the very open, sometimes even wide-open eyes. … They were not staring in horror, as it had been said of him; it was rather more an expression of astonishment. His eyes were brown and shy. When he spoke, they lit up; there was humour in them.' (Josef Paul Hodin, 'Memories of Franz Kafka'. *Horizon* 17, no. 97 (1948), 37).

times when his main characters were suffering the most.[6] There is a Kafka laughter, Deleuze and Guattari claim, '[A] very joyous laughter, that people usually understand poorly'.[7] The filmmaker Stanley Kubrick noted that everyone who called Kafka 'Kafkaesque' had probably never read Kafka.[8] Against the general view of Kafka, various writers like Benjamin, Rehberg, Deleuze, Guattari and Camus[9] have argued that Kafka's work also displays optimism, hope and humour.

This other Kafka is the one that seems to have inspired Giorgio Agamben most and that offers the paradigms that form the fertile soil for rethinking the contemporary political predicament. In that sense, Agamben's indebtedness to Kafka could not be more explicit, when he asserts that '[i]t is a very poor reading of Kafka's works that sees in them only a summation of the anguish of a guilty man before inscrutable power' (IP, 85).

Agamben's legacy

If Franz Kafka is best known as the author of *The Trial*, Giorgio Agamben is best known for his *Homo Sacer*. And just like *The Trial*, *Homo Sacer* gives a gloomy analysis of the current *condition humaine*. Agamben made his breakthrough with *Homo Sacer* and the political analysis he gives in this work dominates the interpretations of his work; the wide diversity of themes he treats, such as aesthetics, language, ethics and religion, do not seem capable of shaking this legacy. His dark political analysis overshadows the fact that he is not a nihilistic philosopher as such and has worked extensively on a theory of freedom, of possibility. Kafka's work plays an important role in his formulation of a theory of freedom.

Agamben's interest in Kafka is both prolonged and comprehensive. The latter crops up regularly from Agamben's first essays in the 1960s to his most recent books, with references to a rich selection of his stories, novellas, aphorisms, letters and journal entries. A study of Agamben's references to

6 Malynne Sternstein, 'Laughter, Gesture and Flesh: Kafka's "In the Penal Colony"' *Modernism/modernity* 8, no. 2 (2001), 315.

7 Gilles Deleuze and Félix Guattari, *Kafka. Toward a Minor Literature* (Minneapolis, London: University of Minnesota Press, 1986), 41.

8 Herr, *Kubrick*, 13.

9 Walter Benjamin, *Selected Writings* (Cambridge, Mass.: Belknap Press, 1996); Albert Camus, 'Hope and the Absurd in the World of Franz Kafka'. In *Kafka: A Collection of Critical Essays*, edited by R. D. Gray (New Jersey: Prentice-Hall, 1962); Deleuze and Guattari, *Kafka*; Peter Rehberg, *Lachen Lesen. Zur Komik Der Moderne Bei Kafka* (Bielefeld: Verlag, 2007).

Kafka yields a remarkable insight: Agamben finds countless examples in Kafka of freedom, potentiality and possibilities to withdraw from power.

That the positive element in their work has remained largely unnoticed has to do primarily with the fact that both have an unorthodox view of freedom and unfreedom. Agamben is clearly influenced by Foucault, who argues that power is not a quality that someone can possess but a relationship, rejecting radically the idea of the subject as a bearer of freedom.[10] A kind of *avant la lettre* version of Foucault can be found in Kafka's work, as Deleuze and Guattari state:

> If Kafka is the greatest theorist of bureaucracy, it is because he shows how, at a certain level (but which one? It is not localizable), the barriers between offices cease to be a 'definite dividing line' and are immersed in a molecular medium, (milieu) that dissolves them and simultaneously makes the office manager proliferate into microfigures impossible to recognize or identify.[11]

It is precisely these ideas of power as a relationship and of letting go of one's subjectivity that not only make power very complex, but also create possibilities for a way out. It is never clear in Kafka's work who has 'power' – the 'powers that be' stay conspicuously offstage. Nor is it clear if someone is subjected to power. Power is fluid and emerges from between force fields. On the one hand, this makes the situation in Kafka's stories even more oppressive but, on the other, it also creates unexpected freedoms. The concept of power and the possible ways out in Agamben's and Kafka's work are complex and thus all the more fascinating. But before we can discuss the concepts of freedom and unfreedom that Kafka and Agamben use, we must first explore how Agamben interprets Kafka.

Agamben's reading of Kafka

Interpretations of Kafka's work can be divided, according to the prominent essayist Susan Sontag, into three schools.[12] The first reads Kafka's work in a political way: modern bureaucracy is seen as absolutely evil. This school focuses primarily on *The Trial*, *The Castle* and 'On the Question of the Laws' as a social allegory of the frustrations and the lunacy of modern bureaucracy

10 Anke Snoek, 'Agamben's Foucault: An Overview'. *Foucault studies*, 10 (2010).
11 Deleuze and Guattari, *Kafka*, 214.
12 Susan Sontag, *Against Interpretation* (London: Eyre & Spottiswoode, 1967); see also Giorgio Agamben, *Remnants of Auschwitz: The Witness and the Archive* (New York: Zone Books, 1999), 18–19.

and its ultimate culmination in the totalitarian state. The second is psychoanalytical and autobiographical. It reads in Kafka's letter to his father and 'The Judgement' a psychoanalytical allegory of Kafka's desperate fear of his father, of castration, his feelings of powerlessness, his dreams from which he could not escape and his hypochondria. The third school is theological. This school sees, primarily in *The Castle*, a religious allegory in which K. attempts in vain to gain access to heaven and in *The Trial* an allegory in which Joseph K is condemned by an inexorable and mysterious divine justice.

Agamben's reading of Kafka is a combination of the first and second schools, but he does add a new dimension to them. He focuses on the political dimension in Kafka's work from the perspective of the philosophy of law and he understands the theological resonance in Kafka's work in terms of political theology. For political theology, many political concepts were originally religious concepts and this results in looking at theological terms in a political way. In that sense, religious concepts play a central role, but their interpretation is profane. Agamben refers to Kafka as a theologian at various times, even as the greatest theologian of the twentieth century, but defines theology as the place where new forms of existence are tested – beyond the animal, human and divine.[13] Therefore, although theology plays an important role in Agamben's work, it is primarily political theology.[14]

In his reading of Kafka, Agamben adds another dimension to his work, partly inspired by Walter Benjamin: Kafka is the author of not only hopelessness, but also of hope; he does not only describes how we are subordinated by law, but also strategies to find freedom beyond this subordination. Above all, in this dimension of hope in Kafka's work, Agamben sees an important strategy with respect to contemporary politics.

Law

Agamben's background in law determines his reading of Kafka to a large extent. He graduated in 1965 with a degree in law from the University of

[13] Giorgio Agamben, 'Vorwort'. In *Die Beamten Des Himmels: Über Engel* (Frankfurt am Main/Leipzig: Verlag der Weltreligionen, 2007), 13; 'Warum War Und Ist Robert Walser So Wichtig?', 2005.

[14] In his analysis of the tradition of political theology, Nitzan Lebovic points out that Agamben's political theology is highly influenced by Jacob Taubes' Paulinian exigency. Agamben, however, takes Paul a step further. Agamben's Paul is a messianic figure who invokes a non-political existence in a *Jetztzeit*. While Carl Schmitt seems to have a prominent place in Agamben's philosophy and political theology, in his later work *The Kingdom and the Glory*, Agamben distances himself from Schimtt's political theology, in favour of Pettersons'. Nitzan Lebovic, 'The Jerusalem School: The Theopolitical Hour'. *New German Critique 105*, 35 (3), 2008, 97; 99; 118–19 and personal conversation.

Rome and then followed seminars led by the German philosopher Martin Heidegger. Agamben himself referred to this as the beginning of his philosophical calling. The legal perspective has always been strongly present in Agamben's philosophy, particularly old Roman law. Kafka had also studied law, even though, according to his biographer Pawel, his heart was not entirely in this choice of profession. 'A Jewish graduate, unless he accepted baptism in order to enter government service, had in fact no other choice but law or medicine, the two professions that offered self-employment'.[15] Kafka first enrolled in philosophy, switched to chemistry, then changed his mind after two weeks and started studying law in November 1901 at the Faculty of Law at the Charles-Ferdinand University. On 18 June 1906, Kafka received his doctorate in law and this familiarity with legal concepts reinforces Agamben's reading of Kafka from a legal perspective. Pawel argues that it is intriguing to speculate on the extent to which those four years of constant exposure to legal prose and legalistic thinking left their mark on Kafka's later work.[16] The relation between life and law will also be one of the major angles to study Agamben's reading of Kafka.

Kafka through the lens of Walter Benjamin

Agamben's reading of Kafka is also influenced by the work of Walter Benjamin.[17] Agamben considers Benjamin to be one of his most prominent philosophical teachers and translated his work into Italian. Benjamin wrote various articles on Kafka and was involved in a long correspondence with the Jewish mystic Gershom Scholem on the meaning and significance of Kafka's work. Scholem reads Kafka primarily from a theological perspective: according to him, the central theme in Kafka's work is the divine judgement of the human being. Like Agamben, Benjamin is more interested in political theology. Although there is also a lot of criticism on the way Agamben interprets Benjamin in general and the way in which he develops his concepts,[18]

15 Ernst Pawel, *The Nightmare of Reason: A Life of Franz Kafka* (New York: Farrar, Straus, Giroux, 1984), 104.

16 Ibid., 125.

17 His reading of Benjamin's messianism is also mediated through Jacob Taubes. Thanks to Nitzan Lebovic for pointing this out to me.

18 Nitzan Lebovic. 'Benjamins Sumpflogik: Ein Kommentar Zu Agambens Kafka Und Benjamin Lektüre'. In *Profanes Leben: Walter Benjamins Dialektik Der Sakularisierung*, edited by Daniel Weidner, 191–212. Frankfurt am Main Suhrkamp, 2010; Vivian Liska, 'Die Tradierbarkeit Der Lücke in Der Zeit. Arendt, Agamben Und Kafka'. In *Hannah Arendt Und Giorigo Agamben. Parallelen, Perspektiven, Kontoversen*, edited by Eva Geulen, Kai Kauffmann and Georg Mein (München: Wilhelm Fink Verlag, 2008), 191–207.

he is undoubtly strongly influenced by his work. It would be excessive to discuss the differences between Agamben and Benjamin in detail here, but it is important to note that this book discusses 'Agamben's Benjamin', rather than it being a critical examination of Benjamin's work itself.

Agamben's unorthodoxy

There are a number of difficulties regarding Agamben's interpretation of Kafka. Two concern his method and use of paradigms and one concerns the practical relevance of his philosophy. Agamben is well known for his unorthodox interpretations of other writers. He himself explains this, stating that he is looking for what can be developed (*Entwickelungsfähigkeit*) in the work of authors he admires. 'According to another methodological principle … the genuine philosophical element in every work, whether it be a work of art, of science, or of thought, is its capacity for elaboration.… [I]t is precisely when one follows such a principle that the difference between what belongs to the author of a work and what is attributable to the interpreter becomes as essential as it is difficult to grasp'. (ST, 8–9) When he develops an idea, he refers, for reasons of modesty, to the original source.

This is not always appreciated and often results in Agamben's being reproached for misunderstanding the texts he refers to because they do not say what he reads into them, as we will discover later on in the commentaries on Agamben's interpretation. What Agamben finds in Kafka is more of a host for many of his own ideas than a hidden teaching about freedom that he can draw from the latter's works.

A second difficulty arises from Agamben's academic method. Agamben uses historical phenomena, such as the state of exception and the *homo sacer*, not in a historical way but as paradigms. A paradigm constructs a certain relationship between two phenomena, for example, between Kafka's story character the 'man from the country' before the door of the law and the legal state of exception. But the relationship between the two phenomena is not a one-to-one attribution of meaning, whereby one phenomenon explains the other by coinciding with it.

Both phenomena remain singularities. The paradigm places them in tension with each other. The relationship that is constructed is not so much between two phenomena as it is between a phenomenon and its own knowability. The Greek word *par* indicates equivalence or equality of value, whereas *para* connects objects, as, for example, in the word 'parallel', where two objects travel in the same direction without meeting. *Para* literally means 'next to': something is shown next to itself (WP). In that sense, there is also a certain overlapping with 'parable', a genre Kafka often uses (TR, 42–3). Agamben, therefore, is not suggesting that the examples he draws from Kafka's work illustrate his philosophy precisely. Rather, he is claiming that they allow a glimpse of a new understanding when held up against certain contemporary phenomena.

Thirdly, there is a great deal of confusion among Agamben's critics and those who endorse his ideas about 'what one can do in the end' with his philosophy. Although his analysis of the political situation is recognized by many, his indications for a way out are viewed as obscure. Agamben's description of the possibilities deviates very much from traditional views of resistance and the same can be said for Kafka. But what supports a positive reading of Kafka – a reading that focuses on the way out?

Kafka's hope: A way out

'Oh, [there is] hope, plenty of hope, an infinite amount of hope' is what Kafka is alleged to have said to Max Brod.[19] But Kafka makes it evident that this hope takes a specific and subtle form by adding: 'but not for us'. Kafka has an unorthodox view of what possibilities humankind still has against power and also of imprisonment and freedom. Kafka's paradoxical attitude to imprisonment and a way out of this is described beautifully in 'He':

> He could have resigned himself to a prison. To end as a prisoner – that could be a life's ambition. But it was a barred cage that he was in. Calmly and insolently, as if at home, the din of the world streamed out and in through the bars, the prisoner was really free, he could take part in everything, nothing that went on outside escaped him, he could simply have left the cage, the bars were yards apart, he was not even a prisoner.[20]

The line between freedom and imprisonment in Kafka is not as distinct and solid as usually claimed. Rather, it is a very thin line and ultimately, perhaps, freedom and imprisonment overlap. In *The Trial*, Kafka describes this paradox in reverse, when the priest in the cathedral introduces himself to Joseph K. as the prison chaplain, as if Joseph K. is already in prison.

[19] Walter Benjamin and Theodor Adorno, *The Complete Correspondence, 1928–1940* (Cambridge: Polity Press, 1999), 225.

[20] Franz Kafka, '"He" Notes from the Year 1920'. In *The Great Wall of China. Stories and Reflections* (New York: Schocken Books, 1970), 154.

'Freedom and bondage are in their essential meaning one', Kafka claims in *The Blue Octavo Notebooks*.[21] And in 'He' he states that it is a matter of making a virtue out of necessity, letting the necessity be a necessity and escaping, creating a way out, in that way: 'I let my necessity remain necessity. I do not drain the swamp, but live in its feverish exhalations'.[22] As the priest says to Joseph K., 'It is not necessary to accept everything as true, one must only accept it as necessary.'[23]

Kafka's ideas on imprisonment, catastrophe, freedom and ways out are not as simple as they might seem on the first reading of, for example, *The Trial*. The short story 'A Report to an Academy' provides further insight into the type of freedom that Kafka had in mind. The hunting expedition of the Hagenbeck Company captured an ape. To train him, they put him in a very small cage on the company's steamboat, a cage that was too low for him to stand up and too small for him to sit down. At the same time the sailors tormented him. The ape realizes that if he wants to live he has to find a way out. But he does not contrast his distressing situation with freedom: 'No, it was not freedom I wanted. Just a way out; to the right, to the left, wherever; I made no other demands'.[24] The way out is not directed so much to a specific goal, i.e. freedom or return, but is simply a way out. The ape continues his story:

> I am afraid that what I mean by 'a way out' will not be clearly understood. I am using it in the most common and also the fullest sense of the word. I deliberately do not say 'freedom'. I do not mean that great feeling of freedom on all sides. Perhaps I knew it as an ape and I have known human beings who long for it. But as far as I am concerned, I did not ask for freedom either then or now.[25]

What kind of hope does Kafka have in mind when claiming that hope exists? It is not freedom, 'that great feeling of freedom on all sides'. Kafka has something more modest in mind: a way out. But how can this way out be found? In any case, the ape Red Peter concludes: 'I no longer know whether escape was possible, but I believe it was; it ought always to be possible for an ape to escape. … I did not do it. What good would it have done me anyway?'[26] After all, he could be captured again and put in an even smaller cage or be

[21] Franz Kafka, *The Blue Octavo Notebooks* (Massachusetts: Exact Change, 1991), 46.
[22] Kafka, 'He', 158.
[23] Translation Deleuze and Guattari, *Kafka*, 45; Franz Kafka, *The Trial*, trans. Breon Mitchell. (New York: Schocken Books, 2009), 171.
[24] Franz Kafka, *Selected Stories* trans. Stanley Corngold. (New York: W. W. Norton, 2007), 80.
[25] Ibid., 79.
[26] Ibid., 80.

eaten by other animals that are on the boat, such as the large snakes. He could also jump overboard, but then he would probably drown. Flight only means new forms of imprisonment or death.

Kafka's characters do not flee. Joseph K., the man present at the knock on the courtyard gate, the creature in the burrow – none of them flee.[27] Kafka's second Octavo notebook includes an unfinished story about an army division that occupies a city. At the first house, they encounter an old man with widespread wings.

> 'You are amazed', the old man said. 'We all have wings, but they have not been of any avail to us and if we could tear them off, we would do so.' 'Why did you not fly away?' I asked. 'Fly away out of our city? Leave home? Leave the dead and the gods?'[28]

It is not a matter of flight, of flying or running away: flight does not solve anything. Nor can the way out be found through active resistance. The question 'Why do you resist?' is posed in Kafka's parable *On Parables*. Although Kafka knew about the Czech socialist and anarchist movements, he did not think much of them:

> They rule the streets and therefore think they rule the world. In fact, they are mistaken. Behind them already are the secretaries, officials, professional politicians, all the modern satraps for whom they are preparing the way to power.[29]

The way out Kafka has in mind is more subtle than active resistance or flight. It is not a matter of wanting to change the world nor of leaving it unchanged. Kafka sketches possible ways out, but he does not flee the world.[30] Hope does not refer to something that is beyond this reality, infinite freedom or paradise. It is essential, Agamben notes, that, just like all antidotes, the way out includes the poison it is intended to combat (PB, 49). 'Why do you resist? If you'd follow the parables, you'd become parables yourselves and with that, free of the everyday struggle'.[31] The way out is attained by giving in in a certain sense, by not resisting. Thus, Red Peter decides that, if apes belong in cages, he will stop being an ape, so that he can address the academy in his new capacity.

Kafka's hope is not a matter of revolution: the way out is not heroic resistance, not a heroic act or active revolution. Rather, it is a very subtle possibility that is often in front of us without our seeing it. In that sense,

27 Deleuze and Guattari, *Kafka*, 46
28 Kafka, *Notebooks*, 48–9.
29 Quoted in Deleuze and Guattari, *Kafka*, 57–8.
30 Ibid., 46.
31 Kafka, *Selected Stories*, 162.

the way out shows similarities to Kafka's description of the 'true way': 'The true way goes over a rope which is not stretched at any great height but just above the ground. It seems more designed to make people stumble than to be walked upon.'[32] The ordinary and unorthodox nature of the way out means that we often do not recognize it. But once we do recognize it, it brings about essential shifts.

Agamben's hope: Profane messianism and potentiality

The world view that emerges from the work of Kafka and Agamben seems to be dark, but Agamben does not this think should lead to pessimism.[33] Freedom and unfreedom, hope and hopelessness overlap for Agamben just as they do for Kafka. Paraphrasing Marx, Agamben claims that the absolutely hopeless state in which society finds itself fills him with hope.[34] He is not interested so much in apocalyptic prophecies in themselves as he is in the answers they provide for finding a way out of the catastrophic situation in which we live today.[35] Agamben connects the possibility of a way out closely with the catastrophe we live in. Antonio Negri describes Agamben's work as a tension between a terrible, existential and preordained background and the attempt to cut through this. Both tendencies are continually present in his work and, when one least expects it, the first overshadows the second and the shadow of death covers the will to live – or *vice versa*.[36] But the words that Theodor Adorno once wrote to Ernst Bloch perhaps describe Agamben's intention best:

> There is something that all people, whether they admit it or not, know in their hearts of hearts: that things could have been different, that that would have been possible. They could not only live without hunger and also probably without fear, but also freely. And yet at the same time – and all over the world – the social apparatus has become so hardened

[32] Franz Kafka, 'Reflections on Sin, Pain, Hope and the True Way'. In *The Great Wall of China. Stories and Reflections.* (New York: Schocken Books, 1970), 49.

[33] Leland Deladurantaye, *Giorgio Agamben: A Critical Introduction* (Stanford, CA: Stanford University Press, 2009), 16–17.

[34] Mathieu Potte-Bonneville and Stany Grelet, 'Une Biopolitique Mineure: Entretien Avec Giorgio Agamben' *Vacarme* 10 (1999), 4–10.

[35] Hanna Leitgeb and Cornelia Vismann, 'Das Unheilige Leben. Ein Gespräch Mit Dem Italienischen Philosophen Giorgio Agamben (Interview)'. *Literaturen* 2, no. 1 (2001), 16–21.

[36] Antonio Negri, 'The Ripe Fruit of Redemption'. Available at www.generationonline.org/t/negriagamben.html, (2004), retrieved on 12/09/2011.

> that what lies before them as a means of possible fulfilment presents itself as radically impossible.[37]

Agamben sees this movement in Kafka: precisely in the catastrophic situations he describes he also finds a possibility, a way out. But this is sometimes difficult to see. The dying man before the door of the law – is he suffering a defeat or not? And Kafka's main character, Joseph K., who is stabbed to death like a dog at the end of *The Trial* – is he defeated? It is not entirely clear in Kafka as to what extent his characters are free or imprisoned, defeated or victorious. Most of Kafka's stories end in the death – violent or not – of the main character. But, as Camus already stated, 'the whole art of Kafka consists in forcing the reader to reread'.[38] The endings to his books often contain an inversion that casts the whole in a new light and yields an entirely different meaning. What initially seems to be a defeat turns out to be a victory after all. Although the situation seems to be initially hopeless, the reader is ultimately left (in rereading) with the feeling that the main character has found a way out.

Just as the ape Red Peter uses the term 'way out' and not the pretentious word 'freedom', because what was at stake for him was more complex than the duality between unfreedom and freedom, so these terms are also conspicuously absent from Agamben's works (although he uses 'freedom' on some occasions, even if refuting its traditional meaning). The terms Agamben uses to indicate his ways out are, for example, 'making inoperative', 'potentiality' and 'messianism'.

The term 'making inoperative' is actually a response to the idea that a counter-position must be taken, that things must be overturned. According to Agamben, this entails the danger that the same mistake will be made. 'Making inoperative' refers to a change in the relation: existing situations are not changed or overcome, but simply lose their validity.

Potentiality is usually understood in relation to actuality: Something is potential only if it can be actualized or realized. Agamben is looking for a form of potentiality that goes beyond the need to be actualized: it continues to exist in a form of suspension. Potentiality is not only 'being-in-act' but more a matter of 'being-in-capacity', being in potentiality. Because potentiality does not need to change into actuality but has its own consistency, it must also *not be able to* become actual. Thus, in essence, it must also be the

[37] Theodor Adorno and Ernst Bloch, 'Etwas Fehlt: Über Die Widersprüche Der Utopischen Sehnsucht'. In *Tendenz, Latenz, Utopie: Werkausgabe Ergäzungsband*, edited by Ernst Bloch (Frankfurt: Suhrkamp, 1985), 353. Cited in DelaDurantaye, *Agamben*, 16 [translation his].

[38] Camus, *Hope and the Absurd*, 147.

capacity to not do or be, or an 'im-potentiality' (HS, 45). Agamben is aiming here at a potentiality to not be.

The third term that Agamben often uses is *messianism*. Although the term evokes religious and metaphysical associations, this is not how Agamben uses this term. His messianism is a radically profane messianism. He is not so much concerned with a specific Messiah as with messianic figures who are characterized by both suffering a defeat and gaining a victory at the same time. Agamben's messianic figures do not represent a transcendent solution for the problems of this world but make the world purely profane: they show us that things can be accepted as they are with no reference to transcendence.

The traditional view is that the coming of the Messiah would lead to the establishment of the kingdom of God. In contrast, Agamben's messianic figures do not inaugurate a new world nor heal this one. They leave everything as it is, just a little bit different. This messianic redemption is not a radical change but simply a small shift, a shift that does not change the things themselves but only their boundaries. Agamben uses the paradigm of the Messiah because it contains important connections with law, language and our view of time. Reflections on this can also be found in Kafka's work and play an important role in Agamben's development of a concept of resistance, of potentiality. On this issues, Dolar places Agamben between Brod, who primarily sees transcendence in Kafka's work and Deleuze and Guattari, who see it as displaying radical immanence. Agamben shows that the boundary between transcendence and immanence disappears in Kafka's work in a radical immanence. Radical immanence is thus transcendence that does not transcend immanence but shows that pure immanence is transcendence with regard to itself.[39] In Chapter 1 I will further elaborate on this.

Kafka's work also contains many allusions to messianism. For example, the way the jackals welcome the European caravan traveller in 'Jackals and Arabs' evokes strong associations with the welcoming of a Messiah, a redeemer of the people.

> 'I am glad to still be able to welcome you here. I had almost given up hope, since we have been waiting for you for time without end; my mother waited and her mother and, further back, all her mothers up to the mother of all jackals.' … 'Master, we want you to put an end to the quarrel that divides the world in two. You are precisely the man whom our ancestors described as the one who would accomplish this.'[40]

[39] Dolar, *Voice*, 165–71

[40] Kafka, Selected Stories, 69–71.

The Castle is often interpreted from a messianic angle as well. But the suspicion that what we find in Kafka is an unorthodox understanding of messianism is already raised by the following aphorism from his third Octavo notebook: 'The Messiah will come only when he is no longer necessary, he will come only one day after his arrival, he will not come on the last day, but on the last day of all.'[41] The date on which Kafka wrote this work (4 December 1917, during World War I and just after the October Revolution in Russia) suggests that he also viewed messianism in close relationship to politics.[42]

Agamben's goal: Fulfilment of the metaphysical tradition

How metaphysics resonates in our understanding of politics, language and time

What Agamben primarily opposes is the metaphysical tradition that dominates Western thinking. He radically rejects the idea of a true identity, origin or end of things. One of his sources of inspiration here is Aristotle, whose philosophy both lies at the origin of metaphysics in Western thought and offers important seeds for overcoming it, for making it inoperative. Agamben focuses on three central concepts in metaphysics in his interpretation of Kafka: politics and identity, language and the ascription of meaning and time and completion.

It is clear from Aristotle's work that metaphysical concepts inform political decisions. For Aristotle, metaphysics and politics are closely interwoven. In his *Ethica Nicomachea*, he explores what is unique to humans in order to determine the end of the *polis*, of the city, of politics: the creation of an environment in which the human being can realize his true nature. A distinction that often arises in the discussion of the true nature of humanity is that between simply being alive and the good life, between physical life and spiritual life, between animal or biological life and human life. The task of politics is to introduce divisions so that it can be determined what true human life is and what it is not. Do people who live only a vegetable existence have the same rights as others? And what rights do foreigners, illegal immigrants or animals have? At the same time, these rights are connected to the issues of identity, of uniqueness, of belonging to a group.

But, Agamben claims, '[t]here is no essence, no historical or spiritual vocation, no biological destiny that humans must enact or realize' (CC, 42).

41 Kafka, *Notebooks*, 63.
42 Thanks to Jaap Gruppelaar for pointing this out to me.

Because the dividing line between the essence and existence of human beings, between the true reality and the manifestation, the body and the spirit is a moving line, each attempt by politics to introduce a distinction here is, according to Agamben, a form of violence. Agamben points to the impossibility – of both the parts and the whole – to coincide completely with themselves and with each other (TR, 55). As Kishik points out: 'Instead of being defined, life always breaks down and divides itself'.[43] There is no transcendent truth, true identity or end of things. Every attempt to assert such is a form of violence and this is exactly what happens in contemporary politics. For Agamben, the human being has no true identity. The existence and essence of a human being is simply 'being-thus', purely as he is without any reference to transcendence. If we accept this thesis, then politics based on metaphysics is meaningless: it has force, but the concepts on which it is based have no meaning.

For Agamben, metaphysics and politics are closely connected with language and time. Language also attempts to give things an identity by naming them and metaphysics has a strongly teleological, linear and chronological understanding of time. Things have an origin and an end towards which they are headed. Another understanding of time yields different possibilities.

Agamben sees important possibilities in Kafka's work for a way out of metaphysics, for making it inoperative. But metaphysics also plays a role in the question of how to interpret Kafka. Agamben defends Kafka against interpreters who do not read his work as a paradigm but seek a true, metaphysical meaning in it.

Kafka defended against his interpreters

In *Against Interpretation*, Susan Sontag critiques interpretations of texts in general: 'The modern style of interpretation excavates and as it excavates, destroys; it digs "behind" the text, to find a sub-text which is the true one', a truth that the author may or may not have consciously inserted and that the interpreters have to find. She is disgusted with the army of interpreters who swooped down on Kafka's work.[44] Benjamin holds that Kafka took every possible precaution against the interpretation of his texts and to ensure

[43] David Kishik, *The Power of Life. Agamben and the Coming Politics* (Stanford, CA: Stanford University Press, 2011), 71.

[44] Sontag, *Against Interpretation*, 8. Because of the enormous amount of interpretations of Kafka's work, I will limit myself to interpretations that are aiming directly at Agamben's interpretation of Kafka.

that his parables would be parables without a key. Much of Kafka's work already contains endless and fruitless attempts at self-interpretation, such as the attempt by the chaplain and Joseph K. in *The Trial* to understand the meaning of the parable 'Before the Law'. But, more generally, the characters in Kafka's works attempt to determine what is going on and, at certain times, if there even is anything going on as such.

In a short essay called 'Kafka Defended Against his Interpreters', Agamben defends Kafka's 'inexplicability'. This short text, the conclusion of *Idea of Prose*, is not directed towards the interpretation of Kafka but discusses, in the same style as many of Kafka's parables, the 'inexplicable' that will be resolved on the 'day of glory', the messianic day. As Liska remarks, the beginning of Agamben's parable, i.e. 'The most diverse legends circulate about the inexplicable …', reminds one very much of Kafka's parable on Prometheus: 'Four legends tell of Prometheus …'.[45]

The first legend on the inexplicable is formulated by the Guardians of the Temple. Their ingenious legend is that the old traditions, being inexplicable, remain so in all possible explanations that have been proposed and are yet to come. The paradox they describe is precisely that the explanations *themselves* offer the best guarantee of the inexplicable. The command 'Explain!' presupposes there is nothing to explain and is itself the only presupposition. It is a command without meaning and precisely for that reason this command cannot be avoided. 'Whatever your response or non-response … even your silence therefore – will in any case be meaningful, will in any case contain an explanation' (IP, 137). Given that there is nothing to explain, the Guardians of the Temple have dropped the codicil that claims that the explanation cannot go on forever and that on the 'day of glory' an end would come to their dance around the inexplicable.

The old patriachs, however, present a different legend on the inexplicable. When they find nothing to explain, they claim that 'The only way to … explain that there is nothing to explain is to give explanations. Any other stance, including silence, seizes on the inexplicable too clumsily: explanations alone leave it intact' (IP, 137). There is no expression more adequate for the inexplicable than the explanation itself. For the old patriarchs, this doctrine corresponds to the lost codicil: it is the day of glory itself, the moment that watches over the inexplicable while leaving it inexplicable. Agamben sees an inversion here:

[45] Vivian Liska, 'The Messiah before the Law. Giorgio Agamben, Walter Benjamin Und Kafka'. In *Benjamin – Agamben. Politics, Messianism, Kabbalah*, edited by Claas Morgenroth Vittoria Borso, Karl Solibakke and Bernd Witte (Würzburg: Königshausen & Neumann, 2010), 170; Kafka, *Selected works*, 129.

> Emptied of their content, explanations thus fulfill their task. But at the point where explanations, by showing their emptiness, leave it be, the inexplicable itself is in jeopardy. Only the explanations were, in truth, inexplicable and the legend was invented to explain them. What was not to be explained is perfectly contained in what no longer explains anything. (IP, 138)

What does this say about Agamben's own interpretation of Kafka? He is not attempting to distil a transcendent truth from Kafka's work; he is not searching for a metaphysical message. To the contrary, he sees paradigms, examples, explanations independent of a transcendent truth that do not attempt to explain Kafka but only show the knowability of different contemporary events. It is thus self-evident to approach Agamben's work and therefore his reading of Kafka in this way, as an inexplicability that is a singularity at the same time, a paradigm.

How to read this book

In searching for strategies to find a way out, we will concentrate on different aspects of metaphysics that we, according to Agamben, must make inoperative. This leads to seven perspectives, each of which will be elaborated in a separate section: the form of the law, life against the law, defining a 'work' of man, strategies directed against activist resistance, resistance to the sacralization of life, our understanding of language and, finally, our understanding of time. These perspectives lead to an array of strategies leading to a way out, to hope. The first section of each chapter will explain the problem of subordination in which we find ourselves and this explanation will be followed by different strategies that can be used against it, based on Agamben's reading of Kafka.

Chapters 1 and 2 focus specifically on the form of the law: a law that, according to Agamben, cannot appeal to a transcendent meaning and thus is in force without significance, without substantive meaning. Strategies against this can be found in Kafka's idea of messianic inversion, in the ruse of the man from the country before the door of the law, in Joseph K.'s self-slander and in Bucephalus' study of law books.

Chapters 3 to 6 concentrate on life that stands against the law and the attempts by the law to determine the identity of life, to make life subjected to law in the double sense: making it a subject and subjecting it. The law attempts to make a distinction between human and non-human life and thus creates bare life (Chapter 3). Strategies against this can be found in

The Castle, where law and life coincide, in Kafka's suggestion that paradise has been destroyed and in his description of creatures – as in, for example, 'Researches of a Dog' – that resist a certain identity or division. Chapter 4 explores the attempt of the law to determine a 'work of man', a specific human activity that determines its identity and should be the goal of politics. Strategies against this can be found in Kafka's own skepticism concerning the possibility of a 'work' as a writer, in Odradek's being without purpose and in the irreparability of the assistants. Sancho Panza's rescue of Dulcinea shows what the saving of humankind from its 'work' could look like. Chapter 5 describes strategies that go contrary to the compulsion for activist resistance, which, according to Agamben, only preserves metaphysical views. Subtler forms of resistance can be found in Kafka's work: in the gestures of the actors in the Oklahoma theatre, a theatre in which everyone can participate, in Joseph K.'s shame and in acting 'as not', as proposed in the parable 'On Parables'. Chapter 6, finally, describes strategies against the attempt of the law to sacralize life, to turn it into the highest good, but at the same time to place it outside the order of law and to abandon it. An answer to this can be found in Kafka's limbo, in the steps of the land surveyor and in the new Kabbalah that Kafka proposes that offers redemption for Klamm and God.

Chapter 7 focuses on the metaphysical presuppositions that can be detected in our understanding of language and that cause the structure of language to deteriorate into presupposition and exclusion. Kafka's description of the return of the person in suspended animation, his idea of impatience, the relation between a name and the unexpressed aspect of the essence of a creature and the justice of the officer in the penal colony offer points of contact for coming to an understanding of the actual meaning of language.

Chapters 8 and 9 addresses our metaphysical view of time, which results in chronological compulsion. Alternatives for this can be found in Kafka's tragic heroes, whose ground of existence is a real nihilism; in Benjamin's interpretation of Kafka's work as the force of untransmissability instead of trying to reveal a transcendent truth; in the *Nachleben* of Odradek; in the closed fist that adorns the city's coat-of-arms; in the free life that Kafka describes in the shadow of the Chinese wall; in the lightness of the bucket rider; and in Kafka's image of the Messiah who comes a day too late.

Finally, the conclusion provides an overview of what Agamben's interpretation of Kafka's work has to offer us.

1

Strategies in Response to Law (1)

One of the peculiar characteristics of Kafka's allegories is that at their very end they contain a possibility of an about-face that completely upsets their meaning.

(MS, 173)

Introduction

In our contemporary democratic Western society, we tend to see the law as an agreement between citizens who want to create a just society. Laws are meant to protect us against violence of our fellow citizens. But Agamben points out that Kafka's work presents us with other insights into the nature of law. Kafka's law is ominously present, but its content is unclear; it is in force, but it has no significance, no substantive meaning. This makes it especially hard in Kafka's universe to distinguish between innocence and guilt, between the law and its violation. Benjamin was the first to describe a link between Kafka's image of the law and a 'state of exception', but Agamben takes this one step further and links it to Carl Schmitt's political notion of the state of exception and sees a strong parallel with our contemporary political situation. The form of law that Kafka describes is not a malfunction of the law, but is intrinsic to it. It is caused by a presupposition in the roots of the law, which results in the fact that law does not protect us but abandons us to legal violence. Moreover, this state of law is becoming increasingly dominant in our contemporary political society, if not to say permanent. In the first section, 'The law that is in force without significance', these new insights in the structure of law that Kafka's work offers us according to Agamben will be described.

Kafka's genius does not lie only in the fact that he portrayed the structure of law in a very clear way. His work also offers various strategies in response to this structure of law. That notwithstanding, the first strategy, 'Kafka's messianic inversion', is also highly indebted to Benjamin. Benjamin links Kafka's work not only to the state of exception, but also to messianism. Secondly, Benjamin describes a kind of doubling, or inversion, which changes the whole situation. Agamben sees this doubling in the state of exception which turns into a real state of exception, the nihilism of the law which turns into a perfect nihilism and the doubling of the figure of the Messiah, who on the one hand is defeated and on the other hand arises anew. This inversion occurs precisely in the most hopeless situations, in the most dehumanizing conditions created by law. But what does this messianic inversion looks like? This will be discussed in detail in Chapter 2.

The law that is in force without significance

According to Agamben, Kafka's work is in the first place important because it shows us new insights into the structure of the law. Agamben describes three features of the law that Kafka's work highlights and that are tightly intertwined: the law as being in force without significance, as a state of exception and as pure judgement.

Being in force without significance

Maybe the most striking aspect of Kafka's law is that its content remains unknown, although different protagonists of his stories try to unravel it. In *The Trial*, Joseph K. is arrested one morning and sometime later, after various complications in his search for the reason of this arrest, is finally stabbed to death without knowing either the charge or the verdict. In the short story 'Before the Law' a man from the country[1] arrives at the open door of the law. Since he wants to familiarize himself with the law, he tries to enter but is prevented from doing so by a doorkeeper. He ends up spending the rest of his life before the door of the law, without ever being able to enter and know the content of the law. Kafka describes similar experiences in the parable 'On the Question of the Laws':

> Unfortunately, our laws are not generally known, they are the secret of the small group of nobles who rule us. We are convinced that these ancient laws are being strictly upheld, but it is still an extremely

[1] Agamben (TR, 46) points out that the term 'man from the country' refers to *am-ha'aretz*. There were various groups among the population during the time of Paul (one of the writers of the Christian New Testament): Pharisees, pagans and people from the country. The Pharisees' task was to enforce the rules and the purity of the priests and were thus uniquely different from the other two groups, the pagans and the people from the country, the *am-ha'aretz*. The latter were ignorant peasants who did not follow the law. According to Agamben, the doorkeeper is a Pharisee and the man from the country an *am-ha'aretz* requesting admittance to the law.

> tormenting thing to be ruled by laws that we do not know … By the way, the existence of these apparent laws can only be surmised.[2]

In Kafka's work, the law is very much felt as a constant threatening presence, but what it prescribes or prohibits and in what sense the law is actually transgressed remains unknown.

Scholem has described this state of law in Kafka's story in a striking way as *Geltung ohne Bedeutung*, i.e. being in force without significance.[3] Kafka talks about a law that *is in force* but does not *signify* anything.[4] This being in force without significance coheres closely with what Scholem called 'the nothing of revelation' (*Nichts der Offenbarung*). Kafka's world is one of revelation, but what it reveals is 'the nothing', the lack of significance, the lack of transcendent meaning.

Agamben sees a correspondence between Kafka's law as 'being in force without significance' and a Kabbalistic[5] interpretation of the original Jewish law, the Torah. These interpretations contend that the original Law was not a fixed text but merely the totality of possible combinations of the Hebrew alphabet. God arranged the letters into words, but their order depended on how the lower world took shape. The Torah took a certain form because of Adam's sin, but the same letters could just as easily have been arranged differently. That is why the Torah has no vowels, punctuation, or accents; it is an allusion to the Torah that was originally nothing more than a heap of unordered letters. Although the Kabbalists never stated it that crudely, the Torah, the Law, was actually put together via a 'medley of letters without order and articulation', i.e., without significance (MS, 165). The original form of the law in Kafka is a command that commands nothing: 'The court does not want anything from you. It receives you when you come and dimisses you when you go'.[6]

What is decisive, according to Agamben, is that this law that no longer has any significance does vanish, yet stays in force. The law is revealed as a nothing and this 'nothing' is not simply an abolishment but a nothing that is still in force. The law is 'reduced to the zero point of its significance, which is, nevertheless, in force as such' (HS, 51). Agamben calls this 'imperfect

2 Kafka, *Selected Stories*, 129–30.

3 The German *Bedeutung* is quite difficult to translate. In the general translations of Agamben's work this is translated with 'significance'. The downside of the use of 'significance' is that it can be interpreted as that the law has no importance, but what is meant is that the law is even the more inevitable because of its lack of substantive meaning.

4 Benjamin and Scholem, *Correspondence*, 142.

5 It must be noted here that this is not part of the 'official' Kabbalistic tradition, but a stream in mystic Jewish thinking that Agamben further develops.

6 Franz Kafka, *The Trial*, trans. Breon Mitchell (New York: Schocken Books, 2009), 160.

nihilism': the law is declared to be no longer significant, but the Nothing is preserved in an eternal and infinitely postponed stated of being in force (MS, 171).

This 'being in force without significance' makes the law invincible. If law does not prescribe anything, then innocence cannot be determined either and the law is always right. An example of this can be found in *The Trial*. 'Look, Willem', says one of the officials that comes to arrest Joseph K. to his partner, 'he admits he doesn't know the law and at the same time claims he's innocent'.[7] It is impossible to master the law precisely because it does not prescribe anything (HS, 58). Another example of how difficult it is to deal with such a law can be found in Kafka's short story 'Before the Law'. Here, the man from the country seeks entrance into the gate of law, but is stopped by a doorkeeper. Remarkably, the door is open and the man bends over to look inside. But what he sees does not seem worth mentioning in the story, as if, Agamben suggests, there is nothing behind the door. The doorkeeper laughs at the curiosity of the man and says that behind the door are only more doorkeepers. So this being in force of the law 'no longer mirror[s] any comprehensible ethical content: the being-in-force is truly meaningless, much as the countenance of the guardian of the law in Kafka's parable is inscrutable' (MWE, 133).

The law is not simply absent or present; rather, it is unrealizable (HS, 51). Because it has no content, this law cannot be abolished. Just like the door in Kafka's parable, it is absolutely impossible to master this being in force by overthrowing it. And one of the pressing risks is that we do not acknowledge this nihilism of the law enough and try to keep finding a transcendent meaning behind the law and by doing so obtain the being in force of the law without content.

> What threatens thinking here is the possibility that thinking might find itself condemned to infinite negotiations with the doorkeeper or, even worse, that it might end by itself assuming the role of the doorkeeper who, without really blocking the entry, shelters the Nothing onto which the door opens.[8]

Agamben sees the law that is 'in force without significance' as a paradigm, a form of law he finds in Kafka, in the Kabbalistic views of the law and, above all, in our contemporary political situation. 'No other formula better expresses the conception of law that our age confronts and cannot master' (MS, 170). Although we tend to think about our law as having some kind of

[7] Ibid., 9.
[8] Ibid., 54.

transcendent meaning, in reality the expression 'in force without significance' seems to be more appropriate to describe our law, according to Agamben. The flaws of the law will be further exposed in the next chapters; for now, I will only highlight one specific feature of the law that Agamben sees closely related to Scholem's description of the law as 'being in force without significance': the state of exception, or the political emergency measure.

The state of exception

In his theses on history, Benjamin describes the times we are living in as a 'state of exception'.[9] Although it is not very clear in Benjamin's short theses what he means by this, Agamben links it to the work of the Nazi jurist Carl Schmitt on this legal category.[10,11] What happens in the state of exception bears strong resemblance with Kafka's law that is in force without significance.

Declaring a state of exception is an emergency measure that can be used if a government is threatened by armies from another country, or rebels within its own country. It is a legal means for suspending the law, precisely with the aim of protecting it, a matter of 'necessity knows no law'. Agamben quotes from the constitution written after the French Revolution (22 Frimaire of the year VIII, art. 92):

9 Benjamin, *Selected Writings 4*, 396.

10 While investigating the archives in connection with the translation of Benjamin's work into Italian, Agamben found a letter from Benjamin to Carl Schmitt. The relationship between these two is a matter of controversy. Benjamin, who committed suicide in 1940 at the France–Spain border in order to escape the Nazis, wrote an admiring letter to the Nazi jurist Schmitt in 1930. Agamben points out that Benjamin's view of the intrinsic relation between law and violence, as he describes it in *Zur Kritik der Gewalt*, has influenced Schmitt's understanding of the state of exception. Violence is usually described as the situation that precedes law, but Benjamin claims that violence is the law's foundation. The law posits itself through legislative violence (*rechtsetzende Gewalt*) and maintains itself through violence that preserves law (*rechtershaltende Gewalt*). This gives law a fundamentally pre-legal, mythical, violent identity, which, according to Benjamin, is precisely the type of law Kafka exposes. See also Salzani, 'The Sentence is the Goal'; Eduardo Zorita, 'Para Una Lectura Critica De Hacia La Critica De La Violencia De Walter Benjamin: Schmitt, Kafka, Agamben'. *Isegoria*, no. 41 (2009): 267–76 and Catherine Mills, *The Philosophy of Agamben* (Stocksfield, UK: Acumen, 2008).

11 Lebovic points out that the way Agamben interprets Benjamin, by linking his concepts to those of Schmitt, creates a new category of Benjamin-interpretations that focus on a critique of biopolitics, but which is not necessarily true to the intellectual history of Benjamin's concepts. These interpretations focus more on a kind of post-Benjamin-theory (Schmitt, Heidegger and Foucault). So in that sense it is maybe better to refer here to a 'post-Benjamin', or 'Agamben's-Benjamin' rather than Benjamin's work itself. Lebovic, 'Benjamins Sumpflogik', 191; 198.

> In the case of armed revolt or disturbance that would threaten the security of the State, the law can, in the places and for the time that it determines, suspend the rule of the constitution. (SE, 5)

In a similar fashion, Hitler declared a state of exception after the Reichstag fire in Berlin in 1933 that lasted 12 years. This was also how Mubarak could rule Egypt for 30 years and how the Bush government reacted on the attack on the Twin Towers in 2001 by declaring a *War on Terrorism*, creating 'places of exception' such as Guantánamo Bay and the Abu Ghraib prison.

In his concept of the state of exception, Agamben elaborates on Carl Schmitt, who saw a close connection between the state of exception and sovereign power. The one who makes the decision about the state of exception is the sovereign power. Therefore, what is obtained in the state of exception is no longer democracy but sovereign power. What characterizes the state of exception is the fact that the law is preserved in its suspension; its content has been removed – to do everything necessary to protect justice – but it is in force all the more. The state of exception is nothing other than a state of law without significance that is in force.

Agamben argues that the state of exception is not something extraordinary (an exception) but is determinative of the structure of our politics as such and is always latently present. The state of exception is often seen as a factual matter, an emergency measure and not as an authentic legal question – as the underlying structure of our law. Agamben's concern is caused by the fact that the state of exception is increasingly becoming the dominant government paradigm in contemporary politics:

> And all power, whether democratic or totalitarian, traditional or revolutionary, has entered into a legitimation crisis in which the state of exception, which was the hidden foundation of the system, has fully come to light. (MS, 170)

We are heading for a global state of exception in which the law is in force but has no significance.[12] As Benjamin already argued, 'The tradition of the oppressed teaches us that the "state of exception" in which we live is the rule.'[13] All this leads Agamben to conclude that, with respect to our political situation, it would be better not to define our political situation in terms of a social contract and civil rights. Rather, it should be defined in terms of a state of exception, a being in force without significance, sovereign power and bare life.

12 DeCauter, *Bloedige Mystificaties*, 10.

13 Walter Benjamin, *Selected Writings 4* (Cambridge, MA: Belknap Press, 1996), 392; translation slightly modified by Agamben.

Law as pure judgement

In *The Time that Remains*, Agamben elaborates further on the characteristics of law in the state of exception. In the state of exception there is absolutely no distinction possible between being within and being outside the law. In other words, there is no longer any 'outside the law'; law includes what it also excludes. If the law includes that which it rejects, then it is impossible to distinguish between keeping the law and breaking it. This makes it impossible to formulate the law: law no longer has the form of a prescription or a prohibition, it is pure judgement (TR, 105). Agamben nowhere defines what he understands by law and, as Salzani remarks, his conclusions regarding law also seem to extend to all regulatory and normative aspects of cultural and social life.[14] In many respects, this is beautifully illustrated in Kafka's *The Trial*.

The usual view of law is that there are rules and if they are broken, a verdict is formulated via a trial and the severity of the punishment is determined on the basis of the seriousness of the offence. Kafka's universe deviates from this in a number of respects. As stated earlier, the content of law remains unknown in Kafka's prose; it is a being in force without significance. As a result, the relationship between trial and law is also different. In *The Trial*, law appears solely in the form of a trial. In Agamben's view, this provides deep insight into the nature of law. Law does not deal with rules and their application but with judgement and therefore the trial. The judgement is an end in itself and this constitutes the mystery of the trial (RA, 18–19). The ultimate end of every legal order is to produce a judgement, but where we tend to think that this judgement strives to punish or praise, seek justice or prove the truth, it is in fact an end in itself: 'The law is only the knowledge of guilt, a trial in the Kafkaesque sense of the term, a perpetual self-accusation without a precept' (TR, 108). In *The Trial*, law and judgement converge and thus also, in a certain sense, law and violence. Agamben points out that 'the essence of the law – of every law – is the trial' and that 'all right (and morality that is contaminated by it) is only tribunal right'; this results in the fact that our categories of law, 'innocence and guilt, obedience and disobedience all become indistinct and lose their importance' (RA, 19). As Grözinger states: in Kafka, human life is nothing more than an ongoing trial.[15]

Agamben refers back to Benjamin to point out that this law as judgement has strong similarities with the form of law in the state of exception. While

[14] Carlo Salzani, '"The Sentence is the Goal": Agamben's Notion of Law'. In *Law, Morality and Power: Global Perspectives on Violence and the State*, edited by Stephen King, Carlo Salzani and Owen Staley (Freeland: The Inter-Disciplinary Press, 2010), 3.

[15] Karl-Erich Grözinger, *Kafka and Kabbalah* (New York: Continuum, 1994), 61.

Scholem views the divine judgement on humankind as the central theme in Kafka's work, Benjamin points out that this judgement does not occur at the end of time but at every single moment. In his 'Reflections on Pain, Sin, Hope and the True Way', Kafka states:

> Only our concept of Time makes it possible for us to call the day of the Last Judgement by that name; in reality it is a summary court in perpetual session [*Standrecht*].[16]

This aphorism reinforces the idea that we live in a state of exception all the more: *Standrecht*, summary judgement, is the law that is in force in the state of exception. In Benjamin's view, this aphorism is connected to an apocryphal gospel: 'Where I meet someone, there will I judge him.'[17] According to this gospel, there is no difference between the Day of Judgement and other days: every day is a perpetual Day of Judgement (MS, 160).

It is important to understand that Agamben uses the state of exception as a paradigm, a singularity through which we can look anew to the structure of the law as described by Kafka or Benjamin and as experienced in our contemporary situation. In that sense, most scholars find Agamben's work useful as a new perspective. So what can be done against this structure of law as 'being in force without significance'? In the next section one overarching strategy will be described to make this structure of law inoperative: Kafka's messianistic inversion. In the next chapter it will be shown how this is embodied in Kafka's stories: in the ruse of the man from the country, the self-slander of Joseph K. and Bucephalus' study.

Kafka's messianic inversion

From imperfect nihilism to perfect nihilism

The picture that Agamben has sketched so far does not sound optimistic: law is in a state of imperfect nihilism, it is in force without significance and exactly this capacity makes law invincible. We seem to have reached an impasse here, a dead point. [18] Agamben shows that if we walk this dead alley to the end, experience the nihilism to the limit, the impasse can become a turning point.

16 Franz Kafka, 'Reflections on Sin, Pain, Hope and the True Way'. In *The Great Wall of China. Stories and Reflections* (New York: Schocken Books, 1970), 287.

17 Cited in Benjamin, *Selected Writings 4*, 407.

18 Benjamin already remarked that Kafka's reflections on law are 'the point where his work comes to a standstill' (Benjamin and Scholem, *Correspondence*, 135).

Let us return to Kafka's description of the law as a constant judgement. What Agamben finds remarkable is that Benjamin provides a description of the messianic time, the judgement day, by making use of a term that is closely related to the term used by Carl Schmitt to describe sovereign power (*Standrecht*). This puts Agamben on the trail of a close relationship between the state of exception (in which sovereign power prevails) and messianism (MS, 162). The contemporary state of exception is not only a state of legal lawlessness, but also contains a messianic possibility. Benjamin summarized this nicely in his eighth thesis in *On the Concept of History*:

> The tradition of the oppressed teaches us that the 'state of exception' in which we live is the rule. We must arrive at a concept of history that corresponds to this fact. Then we will have the production of a *real* state of exception before us as a task.[19]

Our messianic task is, according to Agamben, to bring about a real state of exception, one that will go beyond the being in force without significance of the law, that will not preserve the Nothing in an eternally and infinitely postponed state of being in force. Neither do we want to search for a new transcendent meaning of the law. We need to acknowledge the nihilism without allowing the law's being in force to survive beyond its significance. Agamben calls this a perfect nihilism. This nihilism 'succeeds in finding redemption in the overturning of the Nothing' (MS, 171).[20] Agamben sees this 'inversion' occurring in many of Kafka's parables: an inversion of imperfect nihilism into perfect nihilism, or the virtual state of exception into a real state of exception.

How to restore an empty law: Just a small inversion

At first glance, this emphasis on messianism seems to be a far-fetched solution that is far too simplistic. The idea that a Messiah will appear at the end of all time and will solve all problems is, for many people, an unsatisfactory solution to the political problems of the present time. But Agamben points out that the Messiah was the figure *par excellence* through which the great monotheistic religions attempted to solve the problem of law. For Judaism, Christianity and Shi'ite Islam, His coming meant the fulfillment and complete consummation of the law (HS, 56). According to Agamben, the essential characteristic of messianism is its special relation to law and

[19] Ibid., 392; translation slightly modified by Agamben.

[20] 'Perfect nihilism' is a term that makes clear that no new meaning is searched for, but that the former nihilism is overcome by pushing it to its limit.

the administration of justice (MS, 163). Given this, a study of messianism could provide interesting answers for our contemporary problems with law.

In Jewish tradition, the divine purpose of the Torah, the Law, will be revealed at the coming of the Messiah (MS, 165). God will annul the present combination of the letters and words that now form the law and combine them into new words that will form new sentences and speak about new things. We saw above that, according to the Kabbalists, the Torah was formed from a pile of unordered letters. This makes the relationship between the Messiah and the Law more complicated than at first appears. The Messiah is more complex than he seems because the original structure of the law that must be restored is more complex. How can the Messiah restore a law that has no significance? What is the Messiah to restore? (MS, 163).

According to Scholem, messianism is characterized by two opposing traditions: the restoration of the original state and an utopian impulse directed towards the future and renewal. This leads to the paradoxical sentence: 'the Law will return to its new form'. Messianism is thus not simply directed towards the establishment of a completely new world or a return to paradise. The task of the Messiah is not only to introduce a new law or simply the consummation of the old one. His task is more complex, more contradictory, because it has to resolve the problem of the original structure of the law (MS, 167).

From the above it appears that, for Agamben, messianism is not something that differs radically from the catastrophe in which we live but is actually closely connected with it, almost indistinguishable from it. Or even stronger, the catastrophe enables the redemption, rather than blocking it: only in the burning house can one see the problems in its architecture.

There is a parable about the indistinguisability between the catastrophe and the redemption that Scholem told Benjamin and that Benjamin retells in the following way:

> The *Hassidim* tell a story about the world to come that says everything there will be just as it is here. Just as our room is now, so it will be in the world to come; where our baby sleeps now, there too it will sleep in the other world. And the clothes we wear in this world, those too we will wear there. Everything will be as it is now, just a little different. (Quoted in CC, 52)

Messianism has the same structure as the state of exception but is, at the same time, its inversion. It does not offer any solution from a higher, other reality, but the solution it offers is a subtle inversion. Agamben's messianism is, paradoxically enough, not directed towards the idea of redemption by a transcendent entity but redemption towards the here and now – in this and only this world, in this and only this life, it is a radical immanence. Messianism is an attempt to grasp the possibilities of the current situation. The messianic is not what is still to come, but what is already here.[21] The world will thus remain as it is, 'just a little different'. That is what the inversion consists of. This will be discussed further in Chapter 4. For now, the most important thing is to notice the close relationship between messianism and sovereignty and the type of profane messianism Agamben uses. But before we continue to explore the messianic figures Agamben finds in Kafka's prose, it is important to highlight one more characteristic of the messianic inversion.

The defeat that proves to be a victory

Although it seems that the situation of the law has brought us to an impasse, a standstill, in reality, it offers a way out. But if there is this way out, this inversion, why is it that most of Kafka's stories end with the death of the main character and usually a violent one? This is, for example, the case in 'Before the Law' and in *The Trial*: the man from the country stays before the door of the law until he dies; Joseph K. is stabbed to death by court representatives. How can we interpret these deaths in the light of the interpretation that argues that Kafka's characters triumph over the law? Agamben points out that these deaths gain a different meaning in light of the doubling of the Messiah figure in the Jewish (Kabbalistic) tradition, a doubling that is closely related to Benjamin's doubling of the virtual state of exception and the real state of exception.

Since the first century before Christ, the Messiah was divided into a 'Messiah ben Joseph' and a 'Messiah ben David'. The Messiah from the house of Joseph is the Messiah who will die, killed in the struggle against the powers of evil. The Messiah from the house of David will be the victorious Messiah who ultimately destroys the anti-Messiah Armilos and restores the kingdom.[22] Although Christian theologians in general ignored this doubling of the messianic figure, the dead and resurrected Christ bears similarities with the convergence of both Messiahs in the Jewish tradition. It should be emphasised that Kafka was aware of this tradition through the book *Heidentum, Christentum, Judentum* by his friend Max Brod (MS, 173).

Scholem once wrote that the Messiah ben Joseph is a disconsolate figure who does not redeem anything and whose death coincides with the end

[21] Deladurantaye, *Agamben*, 375–6.

[22] Siegmund Hurwitz, *Die Gestalt Des Sterbenden Messias; Religionspsychologische Aspekte Der Jüdischen Apokalyptik* (Zürich: Rascher Verlag, 1958).

of history. Although this view is true to a certain extent, Agamben is not convinced that it holds up if one looks at the role that the Messiah ben Joseph had to play in the role of the doubling of the Messiah figure. The single Messiah had to be both redeemer and legislator, but some only acknowledge the redeemer and not the legislator, while others do the opposite. The doubling of the Messiah creates a situation where both Messiahs belong to this world, this law, this time and at the same time cannot be identified with it. The doubling results in the Messiah both perishing in the completion of history and, at the same time, as Kafka writes, appearing one day after his arrival (MS, 174). This doubling explains why many of Kafka's characters seem to suffer a defeat that is actually a victory.

Agamben finds many messianic figures in Kafka's work, figures that make the world just a little different, figures that transform the state of exception into a *real* state of exception. In other words, they no longer let the form exist without its content, but transform it into perfect nihilism. They are characters who open a small door through which the Messiah can enter, such as the man from the country and Bucephalus, which will be explored in the next chapter, including the different strategies that Agamben derives from Kafka's short story 'Before the Law'.

2

Strategies in Response to Law (2)

Kafka's characters – and this is why they interest us – have to do with this spectral figure of the law in the state of exception; they seek, each one following his or her own strategy to 'study' and deactivate it, to 'play' with it.

(SE, 64)

Introduction

So far, Agamben's analysis of the structure of the law as a state of exception, a being in force without significance is described. This structure of the law is becoming increasingly more dominant in our contemporary society and seems to be so much the more invincible because it has no content, no prohibitions that can be violated. Agamben claims that Kafka's work offers a key to surpass this impasse: a messianic inversion. This messianic inversion makes the structure of the law inoperative, transforms an imperfect nihilism into a perfect nihilism and the virtual state of exception into a real state of exception. In Chapter 1, the structure of this messianic inversion is described; in this chapter, three examples that Agamben derives from Kafka's work will be elaborated. All these examples are highly connected to Kafka's short story 'Before the Law' and the role it plays in *The Trial*.

The man from the country, the protagonist of 'Before the Law' attempts to come to grips with a law that is all the more unconquerable precisely because it does not prescribe anything. What can one do with an open door that leads nowhere? The ruse of the man from the country is the first strategy that will be described.

This story is told to Joseph K. in *The Trial* by the prison chaplain who tried to offer him some advice. But Joseph K. had already developed another strategy when he is confronted by the law's being in force without significance. If law does not prescribe anything but is nonetheless in force, how does that affect guilt? When is someone guilty before the law? Joseph K. developed in response to this a strategy of self-slander, which will be described in the second section. But this strategy does not prove effective enough and he should have followed the advice of the prison chaplain: to stay outside the law, just like the man from the country. This strategy, which entails the study of the law instead of the practice of it seems to come too late for Joseph K., but it is heeded in other stories, namely, by the man from the country in 'Before the Law' and by the new lawyer Bucephalus who studies the law books far from the battlefield. Their strategy of study will be described in the last section, 'Bucephalus' study'.

The ruse of the man from the country

Chapter 1 already briefly summarized Kafka's short story 'Before the Law' as an example of the law's being in force without significance. But Agamben claims that this interpretation alone does not exhaust the story which also reveals an important strategy against this structure of the law: the ruse that the man from the country exercises. The story reads as follows.

> Before the law stands a doorkeeper. A man from the country comes to the doorkeeper and asks for admittance to the law. But the doorkeeper says that he cannot grant him admittance now. The man reflects and then asks whether he will be allowed to enter later. 'It is possible', says the doorkeeper, 'but not now'. Since the door to the law stands open, as always and the doorkeeper steps aside, the man bends down to look through the doorway into the interior. The doorkeeper notices this and has to laugh. He warns the man from the country that there are many doorkeepers behind him, 'the mere sight of the third one is more than even I can stand'. The man from the country has not expected such difficulties; after all, he thinks, the law ought to be accessible to everyone at all times. He decided to wait until he has permission to enter. 'The doorkeeper gives him a stool and lets him sit to one side of the door. There he sits for days and years. ... During the long years, the man watches the doorkeeper almost continuously. ... [H]e has also come to know the fleas in his fur collar'. When the man from the country feels that his death is near, he beckons the doorkeeper, for he can no longer raise his stiffening body and asks him: 'Everyone strives for the law, so how is it that in all these years no one except me has ever asked for admittance?' The doorkeeper perceives that the man has reached his end and so as to be heard even as the man's hearing is failing, he shouts at him, 'No one else could gain admittance here, because this entrance was intended only for you. Now I will go and shut it'.[1]

[1] Kafka, *Selected Stories*, 68–9.

At first glance, this story seems to lend itself very well to a typical Kafka interpretation in which a person is powerless against the law, a law whose content we do not know; all we experience is that it is in force. It seems to be a story that ends with the death of the powerless protagonist. But Agamben finds it remarkable that everyone interprets the parable in the end as an apology for a defeat, for the irrevocable failure of the man from the country in the presence of an impossible task laid upon him by the law. According to him, we are justified in asking if the text allows another interpretation (HS, 55). The justification for this can be found in the conversation between Joseph K. and the prison chaplain that follows this parable. When Joseph K. exclaims that the doorkeeper has misled the man from the country, the chaplain's response is that 'it is the doorkeeper who is deceived'.[2] To understand how the doorkeeper is deceived, we have to investigate one crucial fact of the story further: that the door to the law is open 'as always'. In his interpretation of the story, Jacques Derrida already focused on this crucial point. Agamben claims that it is indeed an important key to understand the story, but for a different reason than Derrida suggests.

How to enter an open door

Let us resume the story. A man from the country asks admittance to the law, but the doorkeeper refuses this. 'Since the door of the law stands open as always', the man peeks inside, but nowhere does the story indicate that what he sees is of any interest.[3] 'The Law,' Derrida writes, 'keeps itself [*se garde*] without keeping itself, kept [*gardée*] by a doorkeeper who keeps nothing, the door remaining open and open onto nothing.'[4] The door is open because it does not guard any special content. The role of the doorkeeper is to refuse admittance, to guard the nothing to which the door leads.

But if the door is open, why can't the man just enter? Agamben refers here to Massimo Cacciari's work, which emphasizes that the power of the law lies precisely in the impossibility to enter what is already open and to arrive at the place where one already is:

> How can we hope to 'open' if the door is already open? How can we hope to enter-the-open [*entrare-l'aperto*]? In the open, there is, things are there, one does not enter there. … We can enter only there where we can open. The already-open [*il gia-aperto*] immobilizes. … The man

[2] Kafka, *The Trial, 157.*

[3] Kafka, *Selected Stories,* 68.

[4] Jacques Derrida, 'Force of Law'. *Cardozo Law Review* 11 (1990), 919–1045; cited in HS, 49.

> from the country cannot enter, because entering into what is already open is ontologically impossible.[5]

The door to the law does not admit anyone *because* it is open. So far Agamben goes along with the interpretation of Derrida and Cacciari, but he sees it as a description of the law's being in force without significance and not as a way out.

> Nothing – and certainly not the refusal of the doorkeeper – prevents the man from the country from passing through the door of the Law if not the fact that this door is already open and that the Law prescribes nothing (HS, 49).

The open structure that the man from the country cannot enter works like an inclusive exclusion: included by the fact the door is open, excluded because he cannot enter. [6]

According to Derrida, the man from the country responds to this open door with a strategy of 'undecidability and deferral[7], which focuses on the doorkeeper's statement that admittance is 'not yet' possible. But Agamben sees a stronger gesture made by the man from the country, which responds to the challenge of the open door in a different way than Derrida proposed.

The man from the country as a Messiah Ben Joseph

Agamben sees a parallel between Kafka's story 'Before the Law' and a miniature found in a fifteenth-century Hebrew manuscript. This miniature shows the Messiah on horseback before the open gate of the holy city, with a window behind the gate showing a figure who could be a doorkeeper. A boy is standing in front of the Messiah, one step away from the open gate and pointing in its direction. The boy seems to have assumed the task of preparing and facilitating the entry of the Messiah – which seems paradoxical because the gate is wide open.

Perhaps, Agamben claims, the man from the country has the same task as this boy: preparing the arrival of the Messiah. But how does he manage

[5] Massimo Cacciari, *Icone Della Legge* (Milaan: Adelphi, 1985), 69.

[6] See also Agamben's work on 'openness' in *The Open*, where he describes the paradox of the openness of the animal as a positive state (in contrast to Heidegger). The animal is 'outside in an exteriority more external than any open and inside in an intimacy more internal than any closedness. To let the animal be would then mean: to let it be outside of being. … But what is thus left to be outside of being is not thereby negated or taken away; it is not, for this reason, inexistent. It is an existing, real thing that has gone beyond the difference between being and beings.' (O, 91–2)

[7] Catherine Mills, 'Playing with Law. Agamben and Derrida on Postjuridical Justice'. *The South Atlantic Quarterly* 107,1. The Agamben Effect (2008), 57.

to do this? If it is precisely the fact that the door is open that constitutes the law's invincible power, its specific 'strength', then one can see that the whole attitude of the man from the country is nothing other than a complicated and patient strategy to have the door closed and to put an end to its effect (MS, 174). The Messiah can come only after the gate has closed, i.e., after the law has been made ineffective.

According to Agamben, that is also the significance of the mysterious lines in Kafka's *Octavo* notebooks where we read: 'The Messiah will come only when he is no longer necessary, he will come only one day after his arrival, he will not come on the last day, but on the last day of all'.[8] If we recall Agamben's emphasis on the importance of the double figure of the Messiah, we can also see more clearly the role of the man from the country. Agamben claims that Kafka probably had the Messiah ben Joseph in mind when he created his man from the country as a messianic figure. This Messiah dies in his struggle against the powers of evil to prepare the way for the Messiah ben David.

Agamben distinguishes his interpretation of Kafka's parable explicitly from Derrida's that appeared a few years earlier. In his interpretation, Derrida focused mostly on the statement by the doorkeeper that admittance is 'not yet' possible, but Agamben concentrates on the last sentence of the parable in which the gate is closed.[9]

> The final sense of the legend is thus not, as Derrida writes, that of an 'event that succeeds in not happening' (or that happens in not happening: 'an event that happens not to happen,' *un événement qui arrive à ne pas arriver*), but rather precisely the opposite: the story tells how something has really happened in seeming not to happen and the messianic aporias of the man from the country express exactly the difficulty that our age must confront in attempting to master the sovereign ban. (HS, 57)

The issue here, therefore, is not to enter the open door (the law is, after all, empty) or to live in deferral. No, it is a matter of closing the door and this is precisely what the man from the country accomplishes. And most interpreters seem to forget the words with which the story ends: 'No one else

[8] Kafka, *Notebooks*, 28.

[9] For an extensive analysis of the differences between the interpretations of Kafka's parable by Agamben and Derrida, see Mills' 'Agamben's Messianic Politics. Biopolitics, Abandonment and Happy Life', *Contretemps* 5 December 2004 (2004), 42–62. But Mills refrains from saying which of the interpretations describes our current situation better.

could gain admittance here, because this entrance was intended only for you. *Now I will go and shut it*' (italics added).[10]

Odysseus' ruse

Agamben compares the ruse of the man from the country to the craftiness with which Odysseus resists the Sirens' song in Kafka's 'The Silence of the Sirens'. Kafka's version of Homer's story opens with the thesis that plugging Odysseus' companions' ears with wax and chaining himself to the mast was a childish and inadequate way to protect him from the Sirens, because the Sirens have another weapon that is more terrible than their singing: their silence. 'It has never happened, but it might not be altogether unimaginable that someone could save himself from their song, but certainly never from their silence.' (Kafka, cited in HS, 58). The narrator of the story suggests that it is possible that Odysseus did not resist their singing at all but that the Sirens, surprised at his childishness, forgot to sing. Fascinated by Odysseus' blissful smile, they stop singing. So in the end Odysseus did not conquer the singing of the sirens at all and the ultimate victory belongs to them, by having Odysseus make a fool of himself.

But Kafka's story takes a different turn at the end, suggesting that it is also possible that the crafty Odysseus knew that they did not sing and used his

[10] Susanne Lüdemann criticizes Agamben's interpretation of the story based on a distinction between two approaches to the law: a Roman Catholic approach, based on an incarnate power, a sovereign and a Jewish approach based on a mediation via the interpretation of the text. Agamben's interpretation is, according to Lüdemann, proto-Christian and oriented to Schmitt. What Agamben does not see is the psychological obsession of fascination with precisely this law. Whereas the internal and the external, the psychological and the political, flow into each other in Kafka's story, Agamben's interpretation reduces everything to a sovereign power. Lüdemann wonders if Agamben himself is not the victim of the force of the law he wants to describe. The same reflection can be found in Alves who contends that Agamben does not have enough of an eye for the subject and interpersonal relations and sees Kafka's characters too much as victims. Obviously, both Lüdemann and Alves focus primarily on Agamben's interpretation of Kafka's story as he gives it in *Homo Sacer*, where sovereignty is central. In his more extensive interpretation of the parable 'The Messiah and the Sovereign', Agamben accords more room to Messianism. Agamben also explores more extensively the Jewish approach to the law, the interpretation of texts, which he views in an entirely different way. This will be discussed in Chapter 4. Lüdemann, on her end, focuses her interpretation of Agamben primarily on Schmitt's theory of sovereignty and pays less attention to an important influence on Agamben's work, i.e. Foucault's theory of the non-subject. Agamben does not concentrate on a psychological obsession of the subject because one of the core points of both his political philosophy and his theory of potentiality is the non-subject; this will return in Chapters 3 to 6. Susanne Lüdemann, '"*Geltung Ohne Bedeutung*" Zur Architektonik Des Gesetzes Bei Franz Kafka Und Giorgio Agamben'. *Zeitschrift Fur Deutsche Philologie* 124, 4 (2005), 499–519; Marcelo Alves, 'Diante De La Lei: O Camponês De Kafka Não É O Abandonado De Agamben'. *Novos Estudos Juridicos* 12, 2 (2007), 277–84.

ruse merely as a shield.[11] Here Agamben sees a close parallel with the man from the country before the law.

> Just as the Law in 'Before the Law' is insuperable because it prescribes nothing, so the most terrible weapon in Kafka's *The Sirens* is not song but silence (…) Odysseus' almost superhuman intelligence consists precisely in his having noticed that the Sirens were silent and in having opposed them with his trick 'only as a shield,' exactly as the man from the country does with respect to the doorkeeper of the Law (HS, 58).

By insisting that the law must have some content, some transcendent meaning, by insisting that he wants to enter the law, by holding up this shield, the man from the country ends the law's being in force while no longer having significance. In the same way, Odysseus insists that the song of the sirens fills him with ecstasy.

The ruse of the man from the country, his messianic gesture to close the door to the law, thereby abolishing its being in force past its lack of content, is the first but not the only strategy that Agamben derives from Kafka's short story. This story and the role it plays in *The Trial* is a rich source for Agamben for distilling strategies against the structure of the law.

The self-slander of Joseph K.

'The court does not want anything from you'

The short story 'Before the law' is told to Joseph K. by the prison chaplain whilst he is waiting in the cathedral for a business contact who does not show up. Joseph K. and the prison chaplain start fiercely to discuss the story: who deceived who? The doorkeeper, the man from the country, or the other way around? Why are the two statements of the doorkeeper ('he cannot let the man into the Law just now' and 'this entrance was intended for you alone')[12] not contradictory? According to Agamben, Joseph K. fails to see the real problem in the story. What is of primary importance is that the law prescribes nothing and that is precisely why doubt about guilt exists. The statements of the doorkeeper cited above mean: 'You have not been charged' and 'the charge concerns only you; only you can accuse yourself and be accused.' They are, in fact, an invitation to self-accusation, to allow oneself to be locked into the trial (K, 21).

[11] Kafka, *Selected Stories*, 128.
[12] Kafka, *The Trial*, 155.

> The door of the law is the accusation through which the individual comes to be implicated in the law. But the first and supreme accusation is pronounced by the accused himself (…). This is why the law's strategy consists in making the accused believe that the accusation (the door) is destined (perhaps) precisely for him; that the court demands (perhaps) something from him; that there is (perhaps) a trial underway that concerns him. In reality there is no accusation and no trial, at least until the moment in which he who believes he is accused has not accused himself (K, 21).

In *The Trial*, the prison chaplain tells Joseph K.: 'You are deceiving yourself about the court. … The court does not want anything from you. It receives you when you come and dismisses you when you go'.[13] That is why he tells Joseph K. the parable 'Before the Law', because it is a parable on this misunderstanding. The chaplain's explanation of the parable emphasizes that the doorkeeper does not know the content of the law either: 'It is claimed that he does not know the inside of the Law, only the path outside the entrance which he has to keep walking up and down'.[14] The function of the doorkeepers, from the lowest functionary to the highest judge, is not to guard the law but to bring people to the point of accusing themselves, in order to admit them through the door that leads nowhere but to the trial. That is why Joseph K.'s hope that the priest will give him some 'decisive advice' is in vain. In reality, even the chaplain is a doorkeeper of the law – even he 'belongs to the court' (K, 21).

A Kafkaesque universe of grace

It is exactly with regard to this invitation of self-accusation that Joseph K. develops his strategy. How, if the law has no content, no significance at all, can people be guilty or innocent? This seems to be one of the major themes in Kafka's work. 'Guilt is always beyond all doubt', the officer in the penal colony states,[15] and Joseph K. constantly attempts to prove his innocence during the trial. But both guilt and innocence seems to be categories that Kafka surpasses in his work. Agamben sees a close connection between Kafka's work and Pelagius' ideas on grace (TR, 123).[16] The Christian Stoic

[13] Ibid., 160.

[14] Franz Kafka, *The Diaries, 1910–1923* (New York: Schocken Books, 1988), 157.

[15] Kafka, *Selected Stories*, 40.

[16] One of the letters Kafka and Felix Weltsch exchanged regarded Pelagius. Felix Weltsch wrote a book on him, called *Freedom and Grace*. At the beginning of December 1917, Kafka wrote to Weltsch: 'Who was Pelagius? I have read so much about Pelagianism and have not remembered a thing – was it some sort of Catholic heresy?' (Franz Kafka, *Letters to Friends, Family and Editors* (New York: Schocken Books, 1977, 173).

Pelagius lived in the fourth century after Christ and held that Christ's redemption anchored grace once and for all in human nature. Human nature possessed grace as an inaccessible and irrevocable good that could not be lost. Grace precedes every opportunity to sin (TR, 123). The church declared Pelagius a heretic and his ideas heretical and held fast instead to the idea of original sin and an accessible grace (via the mediation of the church) that could, however, be lost. Agamben describes Pelagius' idea of inaccessible grace as follows:

> Grace is a gift so profoundly infused in human nature that it cannot be made known to it, being always already a *res amissa* and always already unappropriable. Inadmissible, since it is always already lost and lost on account of being – like life and nature itself – too intimately possessed, too 'carefully (irrecoverably) hidden away'. (EP, 89)

Agamben sees a close connection between 'a Kafkaesque universe of grace' as is present in Christian dogma and 'a Kafkaesque universe of the law' which is present in Judaism (TR, 123). So if the law has no content but invites people to enter it through an accusation and if grace is irrevocable but (in)accessible, what is the task that Joseph K. has stretched for himself with regard to the structure of the law? How does he react to the invitation of the law to enter in its being in force without significance?

Who slandered Joseph K.?

'Someone must have slandered Joseph K., for one morning, without having done anything wrong, he was arrested'.[17] Although this famous opening line of *The Trial* is often quoted, it does not seem to be taken into account in any explanation of the story. Agamben discusses two details in this sentence that provide more insight into Joseph K.'s strategy in response to the law: the letter K. and the emphasis on slander.

There are various speculations concerning the letter K. that Kafka uses as the name of his main character. The general view, based on Max Brod, is that this letter refers to Kafka's own name. But Agamben points out (following Davide Stimilli) that the letter 'k' had a very different significance in old Roman law. Kafka, who studied the history of Roman law when he was preparing to enter the legal profession, would probably have known this. According to old Roman law, someone who falsely accused another of a crime would have the letter 'k' (the initial for calumniator, slanderer)[18]

[17] Kafka, *The Trial*, 5, cited in K., 13; trans. Agamben.
[18] Slander in Latin is *calumnia*, in old Latin *kalumnia* (K, 13).

branded on his forehead. Given this, the fact that Kafka has given his main character the initial K could indicate that K. has slandered himself. The 'someone' who has set this trial in motion is Joseph K. himself.

A close reading of *The Trial* supports this interpretation. Nowhere is it revealed who accused Joseph K. and there is no speculation about it. But more importantly, Joseph K. knows the whole time that it is far from certain that the court has charged him. That is also what the inspector tells him in their first conversation: 'I cannot inform you that you have been charged with anything or, rather, I do not know whether you have been or not.'[19] The prison chaplain says the same thing at the end of their conversation in the cathedral: 'The court does not want anything from you. It receives you when you come and dismisses you when you go.'[20] That means, according to Agamben: 'The court is not accusing you; it goes along with the accusation you make against yourself'. Although his being under arrest does not entail any changes in his life and he can go on living as he always has, he nonetheless attempts to enter the court buildings (which are not really court buildings but cellars, junk rooms and washrooms that, perhaps, have been transformed into courtrooms only through his staring) and to start a trial that the judges have no intention of initiating themselves. Moreover, what Joseph K. anxiously sees being confirmed by the investigating magistrate during the final investigation is that it is not a real trial but one that exists only insofar as he acknowledges it. Nevertheless, he forces his way into the building, even when he is not summoned (K, 2).

The strategical force of self-slander

Agamben argues that slander is the key to *The Trial* and, perhaps, to Kafka's whole universe (K, 1). He elaborates on this via the relation of slander to confession, truth and torture.

Self-slander makes accusation impossible

Kafka is not concerned with forgiveness (as Brod suggested) but with its opposite: accusation. Although theological interpretations of Kafka's work often suggest otherwise, Kafka rejects the idea of guilt in several places in his work. For example, Joseph K. asks the prison chaplain: 'How can any person in general be guilty?' (cited in K, 15).[21]

Self-slander intensifies the question of guilt. In fact, slander is slander only if the slanderer is convinced of the innocence of the one he is accusing,

[19] Kafka, *The Trial*, 12.
[20] Ibid, 160.
[21] Ibid., 152.

only if he makes the accusation without the accused actually being guilty. In the case of self-slander, a conviction is at the same time both necessary and impossible. The accused, insofar as he slanders himself, is completely aware of his innocence, but he is also, insofar as he accuses himself, aware that he is making himself guilty of slander.

The chaplain seems to agree to a certain extent with Joseph K.'s statement about innocence when he says 'The trial itself gradually merges with the judgement' (cited in K, 15). Roman trials began, in fact, with the *nominis delatio*, entering the name of the accused into the list of accused persons at the instigation of the accuser. It is not guilt (which is not necessary in old Roman law) or punishment that starts the trial, but the accusation. The accusation is probably the legal category *par excellence* without which the whole structure of the law would crumble. Slander was viewed by the Roman jurists as the 'corruption' of the accusation and thus of the law (K, 4).

Slander and self-slander call into question the principle that states there is no punishment without guilt. Guilt does not exist in the case of self-slander, or, better: the only guilt is that of self-slander, which consists in accusing oneself of a non-existent guilt or accusing oneself of one's own innocence – and that is the comic gesture *par excellence*. That comic gesture, in which Joseph K. accuses himself of his own guilt, is the first characteristic of his strategy in response to the law, which is based not on guilt but on accusation.

Roman jurists distinguished two obscure forms of accusation in addition to slander, namely, conspiracy between the accuser and the accused (diametrically opposite to slander) and the withdrawal of the accusation (which the Romans saw as a form of desertion). Joseph K. made himself guilty of all three forms: he slandered himself and insofar as he slandered himself, he conspired with himself and because he did not agree with his own accusation, he sought a way out by attempting to withdraw the accusation.

Self-slander is a subtle strategy, the purpose of which is to deactivate the accusation or to make it inoperative. It is not so much guilt as accusation that brings people into contact with the law. Because the law prescribes nothing, it suggests guilt, invites accusations and entraps people in that way. With a false accusation in which the accuser and the accused conspire together, the fundamental access to the law via the accusation is brought into question. The only way to confirm one's innocence before the law (and the forces that represent it: the father, marriage) is, in this sense, to accuse oneself falsely.

Torture, confession and conviction

In Roman law, a confession was equal to a conviction: 'Whoever confesses is considered to be convicted.' The purpose of a trial is thus also to produce a confession and thus a conviction. In the republican era, confession was seen as something that a subject makes spontaneously because of his conscience and in a way protected the subject. But, according to Agamben, in the imperial era, the criminal procedure viewed torture of the accused as a means to elicit a confession from him, especially in cases of crimes against power. The judge would order torture after initial hesitations or contradictions, or even just because someone claimed to be innocent. The purpose of torture was to get at the truth: torture had to lead to a confession.

This link between torture and confession has an almost morbid attraction to Kafka according to Agamben. 'Yes, torture is extremely important to me', he wrote to his friend Milena Jesenská in November 1920, 'my sole occupation is torturing and being tortured. Why? … to get the damned word out of the damned mouth.'[22] Two months later he enclosed a piece of paper in his letter with a sketch of a torture machine he had devised. A few days earlier, he had confirmed that torture was used to extract a confession, when he compared his situation with that of a man who had been tortured with two screws to his temples:

> The sole difference is that … I don't wait with my screaming until they tighten the screws to force the confession; in fact, I'm already screaming the minute something starts to move in the distance.[23]

That Kafka's fixation on torture went deep finds support also in the story 'In the Penal Colony'. The 'apparatus', devised by the old commandant is, in fact, at once a torture machine and a means of execution for those sentenced to death. It is the officer himself who suggests this when he says: 'We only used torture in the Middle Ages' (cited in K, 19). It is precisely to that extent that the apparatus unites these two functions: the punishment caused by the machine coincides with a certain search for the truth in which the accused – and not the judge – is the one who discovers the truth by deciphering the text that the needle engraves into his flesh. The relation between torture and confession is more complicated in Kafka's work than in the old law, because his view on guilt and innocence is quite different; hence the strategy of self-slander.

Self-slander makes torture, confession and conviction impossible

Agamben emphasizes that it is important to distinguish self-slander from confession. It is absolutely impossible for whoever accuses himself

[22] Franz Kafka, *Letters to Milena*. Trans. Philip Boehm (New York: Schocken Books, 1990), 214–15.

[23] Ibid., 198.

falsely – insofar as he is also the accused – to confess and the court can convict him only as an accuser, if it acknowledges that he is innocent of that of which he is accused. When Leni attempts to persuade Joseph K. to confess, suggesting that only the confession of guilt provides a 'chance to escape', K. also rejects this offer quickly.[24] The aim of the strategy of self-slander is exactly to make the confession impossible, not the trial.

In other places in Kafka's work as well – for example, in a fragment from 1920 – one finds the rejection of confession (and thus self-condemnation): 'To confess one's own guilt and to lie are the same thing. In order to confess, one tells lies.'[25] Self-slander is thus a strategy to make confession impossible and thus conviction impossible. The strategy's aim is not to make the trial impossible but the confession. Self-slander is thus a strategy to question access to law via accusation. So if self-slander makes confession impossible, what happens with torture? What role does torture fulfil then?

Agamben sees a close connection between Kafka's story 'In the Penal Colony' and *The Trial* in relation to torture. Kafka wrote this story in only a few days, while *The Trial* was being edited. The situation in the penal colony is closely related to K.'s in *The Trial*. Like K., the condemned man in the penal colony does not know what he is accused of either. Nor does he know the verdict of the court. 'It would be pointless to tell him',[26] says the officer in the penal colony. Both stories seem to end with an execution or a death sentence (which the officer in the story seems to apply to himself rather than to the condemned man). But, Agamben states, 'it is precisely the obviousness of this conclusion that is necessary to call into question' (K, 19). The death of Joseph K. and the condemned man is not an execution, but shows how torture derails if it loses its connection with confession. That it is not a matter of an execution but one of torture becomes clear in the story precisely at the moment that the machine falls apart and is no longer able to carry out its function: 'This was no torture such as the officer had wished to achieve, this was just plain murder' (cited in K, 19). The real purpose of the machine is thus torture in the search for truth. Death, often a consequence of torture, is only an indirect effect of the revelation of the truth. If the machine is no longer able to have the condemned man decipher the truth on his own flesh (because the officer has taken his place), then torture simply becomes homicide.

It is from this perspective that Agamben reads the final chapter of *The Trial*. In this case, it is not a matter of an execution or a condemnation, but

[24] Kafka, *The Trial*, 105.

[25] Franz Kafka, *Dearest Father: Stories and Other Writings*. Trans. Ernst Kaiser and Eithne Wilkins. (New York: Schocken Books, 1954), 308; translation slightly modified by Agamben.

[26] Kafka, *Selected Stories*, 40.

one of torture. The two men with tall hats who appear before K. are not executioners in the technical sense of the word. They are interrogators who want to extract a confession that, up to that moment, no one has requested from him. If it is true that K. has falsely accused himself, then it is probably precisely this confession of slander that they want to extract. According to Agamben, the curious description of the first physical contact that the men have with K. confirms that it is a question of torture:

> But the moment they reached the door they linked arms with him in a way K. had never walked with anyone before. They put their shoulders close behind his and didn't bend their arms, but used them to entwine the whole length of his arm, grasping K.'s hands at the bottom in an irresistible, practised, textbook grip. K. walked between them, stiffly upright, the three of them forming such a single unit that knocking one down would have meant knocking all of them down.[27]

Agamben sees close similarities here with a German torture method where the accused is stretched out on a rack with his arms drawn tightly behind and above him and his hands tied with a rope running through a pulley. By pulling on the rope, the executioner (*quaestionarius*, *tortor*) can cause the displacement of the victim's collarbone. In addition to this first phase, the victim's skin can also be whipped and flailed with hooks and iron knives (a method that can be seen in the apparatus in the penal colony).

The final scene in *The Trial*, in which K. lies stretched out against a stone 'in a very forced and implausible position' (Kafka, cited in K., 20), is also more a torture session that has gone wrong than an execution. And just as the officer in the penal colony did not succeed in finding the truth he sought through torture, the death of K. seems more like a murder than a search for the truth. Certainly, in the end he lacks the strength to do what he knew to be his duty: 'to seize the knife as it floated from hand to hand above him and plunge it into himself' (Kafka, cited in K, 20). Everyone who has slandered himself can confess the truth only through torturing himself. In the case of the self-slanderer, torture, as a search for the truth, has no purpose any more and turns into plain murder. The strategies Agamben describes do not always turn out well and are a question of putting one's life at stake, for better or for worse, to prepare for a messianic inversion, to be a messianic inversion.

[27] Kafka, *The Trial, 161.*

The strategy fails: The reaction of law

Joseph K.'s self-slander strategy is a comic gesture that consists of accusing oneself in the face of one's own innocence. Self-slander questions the place of accusation as the foundation of the law; it makes confession and thus the conviction, impossible: the court can convict Joseph K. only as an accuser if it acknowledges that he is innocent with respect to what he is accused of. If the confession is impossible, torture as a quest for the truth and the confession has lost its purpose. So far, it seems to be a good strategy. But is it enough?

The law responds by making the implication of guilt itself punishable and making self-slander its own foundation. Not only does it pronounce the verdict at the same time that it acknowledges that the accusation is unfounded, it also transforms the self-slanderer's attempt to escape into its own infinite justification. Because people never cease to slander themselves and others, the law – i.e. the trial – is necessary to determine if the accusation is founded. In that sense, the law can justify itself by presenting itself as the guard against people's self-slandering delirium. And even if the individual is innocent – even if no one, in a general sense, can be found guilty – self-slander remains the original sin, the unfounded accusation that the individual attributes to himself. Joseph K. responds to the invitation to accuse himself in a way similar to how another character from one of Kafka's aphorisms responds. In that aphorism, a prisoner sees a gallows being built in the prison courtyard. Incorrectly concluding that it is meant for him, he escapes his cell one night and hangs himself on the gallows.[28]

Thus, slander can be a weapon in the struggle with and against the authorities, but Kafka is fully aware of the inadequacy of this strategy. It is the other K., the protagonist of *The Castle,* who already noted the inadequacy of the approach when Frieda encourages him to slander Klamm: 'That would be a relatively innocent and in the end quite insufficient means of defence' (Kafka, cited in K, 16).

Bucephalus' study

If the law prescribes nothing but invites people to accuse themselves, whereas at the same time this self-accusation is the original guilt and inadequate in the struggle against the authorities, what strategy can then make such a law inoperative? We saw previously how Joseph K. in *The Trial* attempts in

[28] Kafka, *Dearest Father*, 87.

vain to influence the law. Although he tries to show that the law is in force without significance, his entering the law is already an acknowledgement of this being in force without significance. How can this paradox be resolved? What strategy can be developed?

Again, the parable 'Before the Law' offers the first clue to a new strategy. When the prison chaplain tells Joseph K. the story, he fails to see the strategy that is hidden within it. While in his strategy of self-slander he tries to enter the law to make it inoperative from within, what he really should have done was to try to stay out of the law and not enter its invitation of accusation, even in his crafty way of self-slander. The man from the country manages to stay outside of the law all his life and the way he does that, according to Agamben, is to devote himself unceasingly to study – not of the law, which in itself does not recognise guilt, but a 'long study of doorkeepers':

> During the long years, the man watches the doorkeeper almost continuously. … he has also come to know the fleas in his fur collar.[29]

It is because of this study, this new Talmud, that the man outside succeeds in living outside the trial, something that Joseph K. does not succeed in (K, 21).

Study as a strategy

According to Agamben, study is an important strategy for living outside the law and making it inoperative. In what sense can study be a strategy? Study has a long tradition in Judaism as a form of resistance. In 586 BC, Jerusalem was plundered by the Babylonian king Nebuchadnezzar and the temple of the Jews destroyed. Many Jews died and the rest were taken captive and brought to Babylonia. During the Babylonian exile, when they no longer had a temple and were forbidden to practise their faith, the Jewish people focused on the study of their holy books. After the Persian king Cyrus defeated Babylonia and issued a decree in 537 BC that the exiled Jews could return to their homelands and rebuild their holy sanctuaries, 40,000 Jews returned to rebuild the temple. But the religion of the Jews was already marked by exile and in 70 AD the temple was again destroyed, this time by the Romans. The temple was not rebuilt and study has since then become the true temple of the Jews. The Jewish religion is no longer focused on worship but on study. This gave the scholar a messianic significance (IP, 63). Talmud means 'study'; the original meaning of Torah is not 'law' but 'instruction'. *Mishnan*, the

[29] Kafka, *Selected Stories*, 69.

set of rabbinic laws, is derived from a root that has 'repetition' as its basic meaning.

The study Agamben is aiming at does not have a predetermined goal: getting a degree and a good position in society, or getting some valuable insight that can be used to overthrow a political structure. Just as the strategy to close the door of the law was especially hard because the law does not prescribe anything and the task of the Messiah is paradoxical because there is no original structure of the law to restore, so study also lacks a transcendent meaning it can aim at, a goal it can set. As far as etymology is concerned, the word *studium* is closely related to a root that indicates a collision, a shock or influence. Study and surprise are closely related in that sense. Whoever studies finds oneself shocked, amazed and is, in a certain sense, stupid (cf. *studium*, stupefying). On the one hand, study is *undergone* and, on the other, *undertaken*. Here Agamben sees a close affinity with Aristotle's description of potentiality, which is passive on the one hand – an undergoing – and active on the other – an unstoppable drive to undertake something, to do something, to engage in action. Study is the place where undergoing and undertaking converge; it is a gesture (IP, 64). The rhythm of studying is an alternation between amazement and clarity, discovery and loss, doing and undergoing. This combination of undergoing and undertaking yields a kind of passive activity, a radical passivity. Something happens without seeming to happen. Agamben argues that study is pre-eminently unending. Study does not have an appropriate end nor does it desire it. This gives the scholar a woeful air.

At first glance, the students in Kafka's works seem to be of little use or significance. Nevertheless, Benjamin contends that they have a major role to play: 'Among Kafka's creations, there is a clan which reckons with the brevity of life in a peculiar way. The students who appear in the strangest places in Kafka's works are the spokesmen for and leaders of this clan'.[30] Agamben is in complete agreement with this view:

> [T]he latest, most exemplary embodiment of study in our culture is not the great philosopher nor the sainted doctor. It is rather the student, such as he appears in certain novels of Kafka or Walser. (IP, 65)

It is precisely the apparent uselessness of the students and the hopelessness of study that plays such an important role in the strategy they develop with respect to power.

[30] Benjamin, *Selected Writings 2.2*, 813.

Kafka's useless students without *Schrift*

So the students operating in Kafka's stories have an important characteristic: their studies seem to be useless. In *Amerika*, Karl sees a strange young man:

> He watched silently as the man read in his book, turned the pages and occasionally checked something in another book that he always picked up at lightning speed, often making entries in a notebook, his face always bent surprisingly low over it. Could this man be a student? He did seem to be studying. … 'You're studying?' asked Karl. 'Yes, yes', said the man, using the few moments lost to his studies to rearrange his books.[31] (…) 'And when will you be finished with your studies?' asked Karl. 'It's slow going', said the student. … '[Y]ou can be happy about having given up your studies. I myself have been studying for years, out of pure single-mindedness. It has given me little satisfaction and even less chance of a decent future. [32]

Karl explains his problems with Delamarche to the student. The student cannot really help him either; he does not offer Karl any insight in what he must do and even advises him to remain with Delamarche 'absolutely'.[33] Karl wonders where studying had got him – he had forgotten everything again.[34]

The most extreme example of a student, in Agamben's view, is Melville's Bartleby, the scriber who stopped writing. According to Benjamin, Kafka's students have also lost the *Schrift*. This can mean either that they have stopped writing or that they have lost the *Schrift* in the sense of the Torah, the object of study. According to Scholem, the students have not lost the *Schrift* or the Torah, but they can no longer decipher it (cited in HS, 51). Nonetheless, Benjamin's genius is apparent, according to Agamben, precisely in the fact that the students have lost the *Schrift*. Their commentaries on the *Schrift*, on the Law, are notes in the margin of a blank page.[35] Study does not lead to an *a priori* determined goal; Kafka does not attach any promises to study that are traditionally attached to the study of the Torah. According to Agamben, the messianic tension of study is turned around here. Or better: it has gone beyond itself. Its gesture is that of a power that does not precede but follows its action, which it has left behind forever, of a Talmud that has not

[31] Franz Kafka, *Amerika: The Missing Person*. Trans. M. Harman. (New York: Schocken Books, 2008), 233–4.
[32] Ibid., 237.
[33] Ibid., 238
[34] Ibid., 234.
[35] Beatrice Hanssen, *Walter Benjamin's Other History: Of Stones, Animals, Human Beings and Angels* (Berkeley, CA: University of California Press, 1998), 139.

only announced the reconstruction of the temple but has already forgotten it. 'At this point, study shakes off the sadness that disfigured it and returns to its truest nature: not work, but inspiration, the self-nourishment of the soul' (IP, 65).[36] Kafka's assistants are members of a congregation who have lost their house of prayer. His students have forgotten how to write, have lost the *Schrift*. Now nothing stops them on their '[u]ntrammeled, happy journey'.[37]

The study of the horse Bucephalus

But the most enigmatic example of the student in Kafka's work may be Alexander the Great's horse Bucephalus, who happens to become a lawyer to the surprise of his colleagues.

> We have a new lawyer, Dr. Bucephalus. In his outward appearance there is little to recall the time when he was the warhorse of Alexander of Macedonia. … I recently saw a quite simple court usher with the knowing eye of a little racetrack regular marvelling at the lawyer as the latter, lifting his thighs high, mounted step by step with a stride that made the marble clang. In general the bar approves the admission of Bucephalus. … Nowadays, as no one can deny, there is no great Alexander. To be sure, many know how to commit murder … and many feel that Macedonia is too narrow … but no one, no one, can lead the way to India. Even in those days India's gates were beyond reach, but their direction was indicated by the royal sword. … Today … no one shows the way; many carry swords but only wave them in the air and the gaze that tries to follow them grows confused. Perhaps, therefore, it is really best, as Bucephalus has done, to immerse oneself in law books. Free, his flanks unburdened by the loins of the rider, by quiet lamplight, far from the tumult of Alexander's battle, he reads and turns the pages of our old books.[38]

In his interpretation of this story, Werner Kraft concludes that law is set over against myth in the name of justice: instead of taking part in the mythical (pre-law) struggle, Bucephalus devotes himself to law.[39] Benjamin sees this as a serious misunderstanding of Kafka's story. Indeed, the goal is to unmask

[36] Liska points out that Agamben goes a step further than Benjamin: whereas for Benjamin the task of study itself is a liberation, in Agamben the study itself is also liberated (Liska, 'Die Tradierbarkeit Der Lücke in Der Zeit', 191–207).

[37] Benjamin, *Selected Writings 2.2*, 815.

[38] Kafka, *Selected Stories*, 59–60

[39] Werner Kraft, *Franz Kafka. Durchdringung Und Geheimnis* (Frankfurt am Main: Suhrkamp, 1972), 13–14.

mythical-juridical violence and human beings, like the horse Bucephalus, must tame the mythical forces at whatever cost (SE, 63). But, according to Benjamin, what is new about this 'new lawyer', what is new for the legal profession, is that he does not practise law but only studies it, reading in tranquil lamplight. Bucephalus is free: his flanks are no longer squeezed by Alexander the Great's thighs and he is no longer carrying the latter on his back. The door to justice is not to employ law but to make it inoperative – not by practising law (which would be a repetition of the mythical forces, given that law is in force without significance), but by doing nothing more than studying it. 'The law which is studied but no longer practiced is the gate to justice'.[40] Bucephalus' strategy against law is thus study.

Agamben remarks that it is decisive that the law that is not practised but only studied does not itself become justice but only the door to it. The study of the law has no 'higher purpose' – that is why the law has become inoperative.[41] 'That which opens the passage to justice is not the abolishment of the law but its deactivation and inactivity – that is, another use of the law' (SE, 63). This is a law that is liberated from all discipline and all relation to sovereignty. Bucephalus depicts a figure of the law that is possible after its link with violence and power has been deposed, a law that is no longer in force and applied (SE, 63-64), just as the study of doorkeepers by the man from the country makes it possible to remain living outside the law. Agamben then outlines the following picture of the future:

> One day humanity will play with law just as children play with disused objects, not in order to restore them to their canonical use, but to free them from it for good. (SE, 64)

[40] Benjamin, *Selected Writings 2.2*, 50–1/815.
[41] Hanssen, *Walter Benjamin*, 148–9.

3

Strategies in Response to Bare Life

I have established my burrow and it seems to be a success. ... Yet I am not really out in the open.

(Kafka)[1]

Introduction

In the first chapters of this book, law is described as a state of exception, as a being in force without significance. How does such a law relate to the lives it governs? This question is important in two ways. First, to establish the relation between law and life and second to understand what a life under such a law looks like.

Agamben shows that the relation between law and life constitutes the structure of law. From the beginning of politics, life was only included through an exclusion and law had an ambivalent attitude towards the natural life. Any attempt to make life the centre of politics resulted in the creation of bare life – the blurring of the boundaries between private and public life, as the trial held in Joseph K.'s bedroom shows. Because of this awkward relation to life, politics loses its significance and exposes the lives that it claims to protect to violence, as illustrated in, for example, Kafka's story 'The Burrow'. According to Agamben, life under such a law is bare life and since the law has become seemingly all-encompassing, all our lives are potentially bare lives. How law creates bare life will be discussed in the first section.

The other sections will describe three different strategies of this bare life. How can life, which threatens to coincide with law more and more, find a new dimension? How can the indistinguishability of law and life also be an opportunity, as shown in *The Castle*, or in Kafka's students who lost the *Schrift*? How is this given form in Kafka's own life?

How does the reconciliation of the human being with his animal aspect relate to Kafka's ideas on the banishment from paradise, guilt and innocence? What is the hidden treasure here that is both a tragedy and a celebration?

[1] Kafka, *Selected Stories*, 162; 169.

This second strategy will be discussed in the section 'Kafka's Destruction of Paradise'.

Closely related to this is Kafka's concept of creaturely lives, which provide an important strategy. They play an important role against the attempts of the law to make a division between the human and animal aspects of human life. In a certain way, these creatures appear to be outside the law; they do not belong to either the animal or the human world. These creatures inhabit a world of truth that is the focus of Kafka's story 'The Researches of a Dog'.

The creation of bare life

Bare life and the trial in the bedroom

The structure of the law as a state of exception has its origin in the relation of life to the law. This relation can be traced back to the ancient Greeks but has undergone a number of transformations. According to Agamben, the Greeks, whose ideas lie at the foundation of Western politics, distinguished various kinds of life. *Zoē* was simply being alive, a property shared by people, animals, plants and gods. This includes the banal, natural life of human beings: birth, reproduction, death. Natural, biological life, *zoē*, was not an area for politics but was relegated and confined to domestic life (HS, 1). Natural life was included in politics only via its exclusion, in the house within the city. In addition to natural life, the ancient Greeks also distinguished *bios*: the specific way of life belonging to a species: a human being, an animal or a god, i.e. the good life for that species. This *bios* was central to the *polis* (the city state). This distinction has been preserved in the Western idea of public and private realms: life as a political citizen in the city and life as a member of a family in the house.

This distinction has two important consequences for our politics. Significant of the relation between *zoē* and *bios* is that one type of life, the physical, biological life (private life), was originally not intended to be part of political life. Second, it was not that this natural life simply was *not* relevant for politics; it is enclosed through an exception in the original sense of the word: being taken out (*excaptum*: from *ex-capere*). The specific characteristic of this exception is that it is not the case that that which is excluded does not simply have any relation any longer to the rule. To the contrary: life remains included via its exclusion. The law does apply to it in its own suspension (MS, 162). The law is involved with life insofar as the law withdraws from it.

According to Agamben, the structure of the exception (the state of exception and the law's being in force without significance) is the original relation between the law and life. But while this relation usually emerges in times of crisis or war – in short, in a state of exception – and is hardly noticeable in daily life, it is coming to the fore more and more often, with violent consequences. This has to do with the transition of the state from a territorial one to a population state. Managing the health of citizens is now the central task of politics and simply being alive has become more important than the good life. At the same time, simply being alive is not acknowledged as a human life and politics is searching for the *bios* of the *zoē*, the form of life, the humanity of the living being. But the attempt to reduce human life to its biological essence only results in the creation of bare life. In trying to find the humanity of simply being alive, life becomes stripped of all its specific characteristics and loses its value. With this loss of value, life loses its political rights and comes to stand outside politics. It can be easily killed without the act of killing being viewed as a criminal act. Biological life becomes politicized, becomes the main subject of politics and through this same movement is placed outside the realm of the human. This movement of inclusive exclusion between the law and life, which attempts – with the best of intentions – to make life the highest good of politics, surrenders it to violence. Because biological life has become central to politics but remains excluded from it at the same time, the state of exception has become the rule.

In sum, the relation between private life, biological life and politics is one of inclusive exclusion, of a ban. To the degree that the state of exception becomes the rule, the distinction between politics (public) and private life begins to blur. This extends to all areas of our lives, resulting in dehumanization. The line between public and private, between citizen and biological body, blurs, in TV shows like *Big Brother*, for example, as well as in political decisions concerning coma patients or asylum seekers. Life and the law are increasingly converging, a development that can also be found in Kafka's story.

> What makes Joseph K.'s vicissitudes at once so disquieting and comic is the fact that a public event par excellence – a trial – is presented instead as an absolutely private occurrence in which the courtroom borders on the bedroom. This is precisely what makes *The Trial* a prophetic book. (MWE, 121)

Agamben describes this life – life in the state of exception, life under a law that is still in force but has no significance – as bare life. Bare life is biological life that has been exposed to political power; it is a vulnerable life, a dehumanized life.

Life under law without significance

What does it mean to live under a law that is in force but has no significance? What does it mean to live in a state of exception? When Agamben attended a seminar given by the German philosopher Martin Heidegger in 1966, he asked him if he had read Kafka. Heidegger answered that from the little he had read by Kafka, the short story 'The Burrow' had especially made a great impression on him. The nameless animal, the main character of the story, is obsessively digging an impenetrable burrow that nonetheless increasingly becomes a trap without an exit. And, Agamben asks, is this not the case with the politics of Western nation states?

> The homes – the 'fatherlands' – that these states endeavoured to build revealed themselves in the end to be only lethal traps for the very 'peoples' that were supposed to inhabit them (MWE, 138–9).

Various examples of what life in a state of exception looks like can also be found in Kafka's prose and in modern politics. In one of Kafka's stories, a man and his sister are walking home and pass a courtyard gate. It is unclear if the sister struck the gate on purpose or out of forgetfulness, or only threatened to do so. Nonetheless, they are warned by the people in the village, who are 'cowering in terror', that this will have dire consequences. The man believes that everything will be all right. His sister probably did not hit the gate at all and if she did, it cannot be proven. But before he knows it, he has been imprisoned in the courtyard, which very much resembles a jail, with no hope of release.[2] Agamben states that what Kafka describes is precisely the kind of life that is penetrated by law, a life 'in which law is all the more pervasive for its total lack of content and in which a distracted knock on the door can mark the start of uncontrollable trials' (HS, 52-3).

What is extremely disturbing about the state of exception is that this relation of exception is how the law is connected with life, i.e. it attempts to include it in the same movement as that by which it annuls itself. In the state of exception, the law attempts to protect life; the task of the state is to protect its citizens and therefore the law must protect itself against powers that threaten the legal system. But, at the same time, this life has been handed over completely to a legally determined lawlessness. That is why police shot a 27-year-old Brazilian man on 22 July 2005 in a London Underground station. He looked like a terrorist and acted suspiciously; he was wearing a bomber jacket. It later came to light that he had no connection at all with terrorist movements. How could this happen? On 7 July and on 21 July, London was

[2] Kafka, *Selected Stories*, 124–5.

the target of terrorist attacks, after which a state of emergency was declared. This led to a 'shoot to kill' policy beign adopted by the police, which resulted in the death of an innocent civilian. The state of exception is the condition under which the law has both appropriated life and abandoned it, in which people are both protected by the law and delivered into its violence.[3] If the state of exception becomes the rule, this has major consequences for those who live under that law. Agamben refers to this when he compares Kafka's burrow with contemporary nation states: 'lethal traps for the very "peoples" that were supposed to inhabit them' (MWE, 139). It is important to note that the creation of bare life is not as much a demonstration of the power of law, but of the powerlessness of law. In the end, the main goal of the law is to protect the people.[4]

What possibilities does life have for removing itself from the transcendent claims of the law, from its attempts to create bare life, to reconcile the human being with her animal, biological nature? As Nedoh has pointed out, Kafka's characters appear at crucial passages in Agamben's examination of the relationship between sovereignty and bare life.[5] The indistinguishability of law and life in *The Castle* and in Kafka's own life, his ideas on the destruction of paradise and the creaturely lives that populate his stories, all offer important alternatives to the bare life that politics tends to create.

The indistinguishability of law and life in *The Castle*

In Kafka's novella *The Castle*, the land surveyor K. arrives late one evening in a village at the foot of a mountain on which a castle has been built. He has been summoned there to do some surveying, but decides that it is too late to go to the castle and takes a room at an inn. But as soon as he enters the inn, the people in the village start to point out all kinds of unclear procedures that permeate life at the foot of the mountain. In the rest of the story, K. attempts in vain to gain access to the lord of the castle and to contact a person named Klamm, without, however, being able to get clarity on the procedures for doing so.

On the one hand, this situation is a perfect illustration of the state of exception. We saw the sense in which law, which has become pure form, pure being in force without significance, is inclined to converge with life.

[3] Mills, 'Playing with Law', 17.

[4] Kishik, *Power of Life*, 102.

[5] Nedoh, Boštjan. 'Kafka's Land Suveyor K. Agamben's Anti-Muselmann'. *Angelaki* 16.3 (2011): 151.

As long as the law still holds its own as pure form in the *virtual* state of exception, it allows bare life (the life of Joseph K., or the life that is lived in that village at the foot of the mountain) to exist against itself. This story is central to an intense discussion between Scholem and Benjamin about the possibility of reversing the law's being in force without significance. While Scholem sees primarily the catastrophe, Benjamin searches diligently for the inversion of this catastrophe.[6] Benjamin claims that the life that is lived in the village at the foot of the castle hill offers an example of an inversion of the virtual state of exception.[7] In the *real* state of exception, opposed to the law that converges with life, is a life that, conversely, completely changes into law. The absolute intelligibility of a life wholly resolved into the law corresponds to the impenetrability of the law that, having become indecipherable, now appears as life (being-thus). The two terms that are in a ban relation (bare life and the law) cancel each other out at this point and enter a new dimension (HS, 55). Agamben sees the same happening in *The Trial*: 'The existence and the very body of Joseph K. ultimately coincide with the Trial; they become the Trial' (HS, 53).

Kafka's most unique gesture does not consist (as Scholem believes) in preserving a law that no longer has any significance, but in showing that this ceases to be law and fuses with life at all points. According to Benjamin, this law (or better, this force-of-the-law) is not law but life: a life that is pure and only being-thus, indivisible, liberated from the divisions of power (SE, 63). Catherine Mills, an expert on Agamben's work, summarizes this as follows:

> By the indistinguishability of life and law, Benjamin appears to mean that the law is reduced to the ontic conditions of existence and cannot rule over life through claims to transcendence. Correlatively, there is no possibility of interpretation of the law from the position of life, since life is itself indistinguishable from law.[8]

A law without a key to decipher it converges with life, according to Benjamin. Instead of the word 'law', Benjamin also uses the German word *Schrift*. In Chapter 2, we saw that this term is closely associated with writing, law and religious law (the Torah and the Bible are also called *Der Schrift* – the Torah is then the written law). In that respect, Miguel Vatter points out that *Schrift* is a layered concept[9]. According to him, it also refers to prose writings. When

[6] Benjamin and Scholem, *Correspondence*, 127–35.

[7] The following passage elaborates on Agamben's interpretation of Benjamin's work.

[8] Mills, *Agamben's Messianic Politics*, 45–6.

[9] Vatte also criticizes Agamben's use of Benjamin's concept. 'In contrast to Agamben's interpretation, the *Schrift* that is at stake here is the Torah that fulfills itself in its transgression … and not the writing of a new law "that cancels nothing and no form or force

Benjamin states that *Der Schrift* without a key converges with life, this can also mean the law – as writing – converges with life.

It is not only in his prose that *Schrift* (writing/law) and life converge for Kafka; this also occurred in his own life. William Watkin points out Kafka's attempt to create a work of pure silence in response to power and his unanswered request to have his work destroyed after his death.[10] In *The End of the Poem*, Agamben quotes from Kafka's *Octavo* notebooks concerning the relation between and the fusing of, life and writing in Kafka:

> It seems as though he were underpinning his existence with retrospective justifications, but that is only psychological mirror-writing; in actual fact he is erecting his life on his justifications.[11]

Agamben refers to another writer, Delfini, for whom life and writing were fused. For Delfini, no distinction at all can be made between what was lived and what was poeticized. Agamben sees a strong similarity between Delfini and Kafka: 'Their biographical failure (or at least what appears as such in the inverted image of psychology) had to bear witness to – and not justify – the theological authenticity of writing (its dwelling in the *arche*)' (EP, 82). Dora Dymant, Kafka's last lover and the only one he lived together with, describes Kafka's writing as his life-breath: 'The days on which he wrote were the rhythm of his breath.'[12]

David Kishik has pointed out that Agamben's life and work also intertwine: 'if you want to know all about Giorgio Agamben, just look at the surface of his books and essays and seminars and there he is, there is nothing behind it.'[13]

So the first strategy against the creation of the bare life, the penetration of law into life, is reversing this in an indistinguishability between law and life, to make law lose its transcendence over life. This is closely related to how the law's being in force past its significance was made inoperative. The second and third strategy aim at the abolishment of the distinction between *zoē* and *bios* by questioning the special status of paradise and by transforming naked life into creaturely life.

of the law, not to mention its significance". … The writing in which life in the [Kafka's] village is transformed and reversed … is the writing of fiction' ('In Odradek's World', 66). Miguel Vatter, 'In Odradek's World: Bare Life and Historical Materialism in Agamben and Benjamin,' *diacritics* 38, no. 3 (2008), 66.

10 William Watkin, *The Literary Agamben*. New York: Continuum, 2010.

11 Kafka, *Octavo Notebooks*, 51

12 Hodin, 'Kafka', 38.

13 Kishik, *Power of Life*, 13.

Kafka's destruction of paradise

In one of his journal entries, Kafka states that there are three ways of punishing the fall into sin:

> The mildest kind was immediately inflicted and it was the banishment from paradise; the second was the destruction of paradise itself; and the third – and this is said to have been the worst punishment of all – was the barring of access to the eternal way, with everything else left as before.[14]

In Kafka's suggestion of the destruction of paradise, Agamben sees a possible strategy against creating bare life in which the division between animals and humans plays an important role. Agamben develops this strategy by comparing Kafka's journal entry here with a note from the Italian writer Elsa Morante, one of his friends who had been strongly influenced by Kafka.

Agamben has a version of Spinoza's *Ethica* that was owned by Morante and in which she made notes. Spinoza plays an important role in her work, but in the *Ethica* she appears to disagree with him on an important point: against Spinoza's statement that people have more virtue and power than animals, Morante claims that after eating from the tree of knowledge it was people, not animals, who were driven from paradise. Agamben compares this with the above journal entry by Kafka. At first glance, it seems that Morante chooses the first option: people were driven out of paradise; animals were not. According to Agamben, Morante makes a wrong step here. With this definition of the difference between people and animals, she emphasizes, namely, the bare life of beings: their innocence and their extreme guilt. She confirms the distinction between animals and humans, their sacredness and their curse, their darkness and their light. This search for such distinctions results in the creation of bare life since the human and the animal parts of one being cannot be divided that neatly.

But a form of perfect nihilism can also result from this analysis of the relation of the human and the animal to paradise. Morante finds this, remarkably enough, also in Spinoza. She describes Spinoza's work as 'the celebration of a hidden treasure' that leads to more despair than any tragedy and to more celebration than any comedy. This hidden treasure is the divine spark in all creatures: a spiritualization of matter and the materialization of light, an indistinguishability. And here Morante abandons Kafka's first and third options for the second, the destruction of paradise, the destruction of the division between paradise and the world, which makes the specific

[14] Kafka, *Dearest Father*, 87–8; translation slightly modified by Agamben (EP, 107–8).

distinction between humans and animals inoperative. As Kafka states in his 'Reflections on Sin, Pain, Hope and the True Way', it is the certainty that only the spiritual world exists that deprives us of hope and gives certainty (cited in EP, 107–8). On the one hand, this is tragic – the loss of hidden mysteries, of transcendence for pure immanence – and, on the other, a celebration. It is now up to the angelical wild beasts among people and animals (EP, 107–8). Agamben elaborates on a similar theme in *The Open*, in which he states that on the last day, after the coming of the Messiah, 'the relation between animals and people will take on a new form and ... the human being will be reconciled with his animal nature' (O, 3). Bare life will then be impossible; we will all live angelic wild lives. So this second strategy tries to find a new relationship between *zoē* and *bios* within the living being. The third strategy shows what form this new life can take.

Kafka's creaturely lives

Deleuze and Guattari argue that, for Kafka, the essence of the animal is the way out. Everything in the animal is a metamorphosis and that metamorphosis is the animal becoming human and the human becoming animal. It is a deterritorialization on both sides, a shifting of the border.[15] Although Agamben himself never referred to this directly, a number of his interpreters point out that Kafka's boundary figures between animals and humans constitute an escape from the distinction between *zoē* and *bios*, an inversion of the imperfect nihilism of bare life. Santner calls this 'creaturely life', which refers both to creating life and the life of creatures.[16] The word 'creature' refers, on the one hand, to 'creating'; this life is a byproduct, a creature under the influence of the law. Joseph K.'s cry 'like a dog!' points to this influence of the law. On the other hand, the word 'creature' refers to a blurred line between different forms of life – that of people, of animals – which enables these creatures to make the law inoperative for them.[17] Abbott points out the parallel between 'creatures' and the man from the country before the door to the law. Creatures are not only created within the power relation but remain outside of it at the same time. In *Nudities*, Agamben distinguishes between an angelic power and a corporeal power. Salvation will not come from the angelic power, a power that helps humans to produce their works, but from

[15] Deleuze and Guattari, *Kafka*, 35.

[16] Eric Santner, *On Creaturely Life: Rilke, Benjamin, Sebald*. (Chicago and London: University of Chicago Press, 2006), 28.

[17] Matthew Abbott, 'The Creature before the Law: Notes on Walter Benjamin's Critique of Violence', *Colloquy text theory critique* 16 (2008), 86.

a 'more humble and corporeal power, which humans have insofar as they are created beings'. (N, 5).

Agamben refers only once, briefly, to Kafka's 'Researches of a Dog'. He does this in the essay, 'K.', where he explains what strategy the land surveyor uses to make the dividing lines between the higher and the lower, the pure and impure, inoperative (see Chapter 6). But the surveyor is allowed only a glimpse of what the world looks like after these lines have been made inoperative. According to Agamben, however, the researches of a dog are also directed towards this 'world of truth'. This world of truth is full of creatures who are dogs but do not adhere to the laws and characteristics of dogs, even though they are indisputably dogs. In a certain sense, these creatures are also outside the law; they frustrate the line between animal and human, between humans and the divine and denote a threshold.[18]

Kafka's story is about a dog that 'lives like a dog among dogs' and does everything that normal dogs do. But this dog has discovered a flaw in himself: he does not feel at ease among the other dogs. This motivates him to engage in research into, for example, music dogs and air dogs. He describes how, as a young dog in the excitement of youth, he once saw seven music dogs appear out of nowhere.

> They did not speak, they did not sing, in general they held their tongue with almost a certain doggedness, but they conjured forth Music out of that empty space. … They have appeared, you welcomed them silently as dogs; true, the clamor that accompanied them was very confusing, but in the end they were dogs, dogs like you and me.[19]

But they do not answer when the dog asks them some questions. And this is a major transgression of the norms for the way dogs are supposed to treat one another. It seems as if the smallest dog is tempted to talk to him, but the others prevent him from doing so.

> But why was it not allowed, why wasn't the thing that our laws always unconditionally require not allowed this time? My heart rebelled, I almost forgot the music. These dogs before me were violating the law. Great magicians they might be, but the law applied to them as well: that was something that I, a child, already knew very well.[20]

These dogs even walk on their hind legs! The next creatures that the dog meets are air dogs. When he first heard about them, he had to laugh. They

[18] Murray, Alex, *Giorgio Agamben* (London; New York: Routledge, 2009), 100.
[19] Kafka, Selected stories, 134–5.
[20] Ibid., 136.

are small dogs, no larger than his head, who move high up through the air, making no effort to do so but lying on cushions. They have abandoned all physical movement and talk constantly about their worthless philosophical ponderings. They do not hunt, they do not sow or reap, but are fed extraordinarily well at the expense of the dog society. What he finds strange is the silent foolishness of such ways of existence.

When Agamben claims that the investigations of the dog aim at a world of truth, how does that relate to the different types of strange dogs that the narrator meets? These dogs seem to be an intermediate form between animals and humans. These dogs probably offer a glimpse into the world of truth that is possible after the boundaries dividing *zoē* and *bios*, life form and biological life, are made inoperative. Seeing these strange dogs, the narrator dog concludes: 'The freedom that is possible today – a stunted growth'.[21] Real freedom will come after the distinctions between *zoē* and *bios* have disappeared.

[21] Ibid., 161.

4

Strategies in Response to the 'Work of Man'

The whole thing seems meaningless yet in its own way complete.
(Franz Kafka about Odradek)[1]

Introduction

In the previous chapter, we saw that law creates bare life in its attempt to separate *zoē* and *bios* in a living being. Over and against this bare life most people place a subject, a *bios*, a bearer of human values such as dignity. This subject is viewed as the protagonist against law, a protagonist that will prevent the creation of bare life. Agamben tries to show that this subject, along with the search for human values, cannot be the real protagonist resisting power, because it shares the same metaphysical assumptions that underlie the creation of bare life. That is, trying to determine the humanity of the living being, to determine a 'work of man'.

What distinguishes the human form of life from other forms? Aristotle tried to answer this question by defining the specific 'work' of man. Just like the acorn that becomes an oak tree, so the human being must realise his potential. But then: what is the activity that characterizes human life? What is the work the human being must do, or the path the human being must follow to find fulfilment? And how can the human being be 'repaired' if he deviates from his work, from his potentiality? Agamben shows that, through this search for the work of man, human life is subordinated to all kinds of legal violence, exclusion and dehumanization because human life cannot be grasped in metaphysical distinctions and Agamben finds different strategies in Kafka's work against this determination of a work of man and against a subject as bearer of human values.

The first strategy that will be described emerges from Kafka's diaries and looks at his own calling, his own work as a writer and his attempts to make a 'work cage' for himself. Kafka openly struggles with the question whether or not it is at all possible to have a 'work' – as a human being or as an artist. Essence always seems to elude existence and transcendence

[1] Kafka, *Selected Stories*, 72

incommensurable with immanence. The characters in Kafka's stories relate in many ways to the idea of a specific work. From there, two more strategies can be derived: that of Odradek and that of the assistants and messengers. Odradek, who has no origin, goal or specific activity, evokes the jealousy of the father of the family because he seems to be indestructible. The assistants and messengers in *The Castle* who do not seem to be aware of their task or even that they have a task, are other examples of the possibilities 'having no work' offers.

Does this lack of a work suggest that the human being does not actually have a task or work of his own? Agamben claims that this is the case and that this is not a defect that needs to be repaired. Rather, it is in the fact of its irreparability that our hope consists, in the fact that people simply are as they are, that they are 'being-thus'. Kafka's assistants are an example for Agamben of this irreparability. People do not need to be saved from their lack of work (*ergon*) but from the metaphysical political attempts to ascribe a work to man. But why, as Agamben's version of Kafka's story 'The Truth about Sancho Panza' shows, are those whom we love not happy with this salvation?

Determining the 'work of man'

The transformation of the human being in bare life is closely associated with the metaphysical search for the 'work' that belongs to humankind as such. The word 'work' does not refer here simply to a job, but to that which characterizes the actions and activities of human beings, that which identifies them as human beings. This involves the human person being active as a human being, independent of and beyond any concrete social roles that he or she can assume.

In the first book of the *Ethica Nicomachea*, Aristotle poses the problem of defining the unique 'work of man'.[2] This question coheres closely with that of the *telos*, the end or goal of the human being. What is the fulfillment that naturally belongs to the human being and that is reached simply through the unhindered performance of his characteristic function or work (*ergon*)? Or, Aristotle wonders, should we hold that there is no special 'work' that belongs to humankind as such? He seems to suggest this, i.e. that there is an essential inactivity of the human being, that the actual nature of the human being is that of a living being that has no 'work', that has no specific nature or calling. If the human being does not have any work (*ergon*) of his own, he will not

[2] Aristotle, *The Nicomachean Ethics* (Filiquarian Publishing: Minneapolis, 2007), 1097b, 22ff.

even have any *energeia*, a being-in-act that defines his essence. He would be a being of pure potentiality, without an identity or work that could exhaust his 'being'. But, although Aristotle raises the hypothesis 'that there is no work of man as such', he seems to back away from it and continues to search for a work that belongs specifically to humankind.

According to Agamben, the function of Aristotle's search for a work of man is not only that of ascribing a proper nature and essence to human beings, but also of determining their happiness and politics through such a work (WM, 2). Aristotle defines happiness as the activity of the soul in accordance with its excellence and the purpose of politics is to bring about the happiness of human beings. Quite abruptly, Aristotle places the *ergon* of the human being, the work of man, in the sphere of a specific form of life. In Agamben's view, this shows that the nexus between politics and life was present in Greek political thought from the start. Aristotle introduces a number of caesurae into the continuum of life: life according to reason in contrast to simply being alive. What is unique to the human being? Human life is different from vegetative life – which plants and animals also have – and the sensory life humans share with animals. Thus, living in accordance with the *logos* is then the only possible form of life that is purely human. The unique work of man is, according to Aristotle, the activity of the soul in accordance with the *logos*.

Aristotle's definition of the work of man contains, in Agamben's view, two theses regarding politics (WM, 5). First, politics is directed to the work of man; it aims at bringing out the specific activity of the human being. Second, this work of man was originally defined on the basis of the exclusion of the natural life, the non-rational (animal, vegetative) life, from life according to reason. With this, politics have become biopolitics: 'It binds the destiny of politics to a kind of work, which remains unassignable with respect to individual human activities.' (WM, 5). But it is precisely these definitions of the humanity of the human being, the determination of a work of man, that lead to various forms of exclusion and dehumanization.

However, Agamben argues that another reading of Aristotle's idea of the work of man is possible, whereby Aristotle does not leave us so much with biopolitics as with a way out. As Aristotle himself already suggests at the beginning of *Ethica Nicomachea*, it is possible that the human being does not have any unique work. Both Averroes and Dante emphasize primarily this suggestion in Aristotle, i.e. that potentiality is the specific character of the work of man (WM, 7). This is a work that expresses itself in the possibility of its own non-existence, its own inactivity, a work that achieves its own *shabbat*, its own impotentiality, in each act (WM, 10). Agamben finds in Kafka's prose different figures who express the lack of work, their own impotentiality, such as the assistants in *The Castle* or Odradek. But Kafka also had doubts about the possibility of a specific work in his own vocation as a writer.

Kafka's idea of a 'work cage', Odradek's being without purpose, the fact of the assistants and messengers having no work, the irreparability of the assistants and Sancho Panza's saving of Dulcinea, give us a variety of strategies for responding to the attempt to define a 'work of man'.

Kafka's 'work cage'

In one of his first works, 'Il Pozzo di Babele' (1966) – also one of his first references to Kafka – Agamben claims that the concept 'work' (*opera*), is not conceivable without any ambiguity. According to Agamben, the work is predestined to fail and Kafka is *the* writer who has experienced that in a very profound way. Kafka expresses himself critically in his journals and in his aphorisms on the possibility of a work of man. But these references are not concerned with a work of the human being in general, but with a work of an artist, a work that is presupposed to contain a certain transcendence over matter.

When an artist feels confronted by a true essence that he wants to grasp, the only thing he has at his disposal is matter, the fleeting axis of words that never allows him to grasp the essence. If he opts for the essence and rejects the worldly possibilities for grasping it, he then loses the world. But if he opts for the worldly possibilities, he then loses the essence. Here the writer is caught between the work of art and the assumed transcendence of this work: the more he attempts to bind the work in words, the more it escapes him, leaving him with a false representation. But if he wants to realize the work beyond the material, throwing himself into what Agamben calls the shaft of Babel, it will still evade his grasp. This paradoxical situation of the writer in relation to his work is very clearly articulated in a passage from Kafka's journals (27 December 1911):

> My feeling when I write something that is wrong might be depicted as follows: In front of two holes in the ground a man is waiting for something to appear that can rise up only out of the hole on his right. But while this hole remains covered over by a dimly visible lid, one thing after another rises up out of the hole on his left, keeps trying to attract his attention and in the end succeeds in doing this without any difficulty because of its swelling size, which, much as the man may try to prevent it, finally covers up even the right hole. But the man – he does not want

> to leave this place and indeed refuses to at any price – has nothing but these appearances and although – fleeting as they are, their strength is used up by their merely appearing –they cannot satisfy him, he still strives, whenever out of weakness they are arrested in their rising up, to drive them up and scatter them into the air if only he can thus bring up others; for the permanent sight of one is unbearable and moreover he continues to hope that after the false appearances have been exhausted, the true will finally appear.[3]

Agamben sees a strong paradox here between the *desire* to write and the *impossibility* of writing: the paradox of the absence of work as a condition of its existence. He also sees this as the meaning of Kafka's aphorism 'A cage went in search of a bird'.[4] The need to write is this absurd desire to make a 'work cage' out of oneself: a desire that can silence the one whom the desire controls, precisely when all one wants to do is to write. Whoever has felt this desire knows how this can swallow up all other content and thus immediately make the work impotent. And at that moment he is thrown into a paradoxical situation of 'wanting to write with a burned hand about the nature of fire' (PB, 42).

In Agamben's view, what Kafka is describing is a paradox in which the absence of a work is the condition of its existence, in which the work is predestined to fail, but that only this impotence, this silence and emptiness can save the work, reversing it in a perfect nihilism, a pure immanence. Earlier, we discussed a similar movement in Kafka's work in which work and life merged together and to which we will return in the chapter on language (Chapter 7), in which literature is described as a blind alley that must be followed to the end and Chapter 8, in which Benjamin argues that Kafka's originality lies in the fact that he has given up transcendence, the truth, for the transmission itself, the work as immanence. For now, we need only to note that Kafka is the writer who most deeply experiences the predestined failure of the work as transcendence. This is evident from his story *A Country Doctor*.[5] Although the doctor responds to the night bell and wanders through the snow in his carriage pulled by two unreal horses, he appears to have been deceived. There is no work for him: the patient begs to be allowed to die peacefully; 'I once listened to the false alarm of the night bell and there is no longer a remedy'.[6]

Agamben reads in this story and in Kafka's diary entry, a resistance against the possibility of a work of man. Different characters in his stories,

[3] Kafka, 1988, *Diaries*, 200.
[4] Kafka, *Dearest Father*, 36.
[5] Kafka, *Selected Stories*, 60–5.
[6] Ibid., 2007; cited in PB, 45; translation slighty modified by Agamben.

like Odradek and the assistants, show what it is like to be a living being without work.

Odradek's being without purpose

Odradek is one of Kafka's characters who explicitly has no specific work, purpose or origin. The story 'The Worry of the Father of the Family' begins with various explanations of the origin of the word Odradek, stating that none of these explanations can finally determine the meaning of this word. In short, Odradek's origin remains unknown and, as comes to light later in the story, so do his 'work' and his purpose.[7]

> No one, of course, would occupy himself with such studies if there were not really a creature called Odradek. … It is tempting to think that this figure once had some sort of functional shape and is now merely broken. But this does not seem to be the case; at least there is no evidence for such a speculation; nowhere can you see any other beginnings or fractures that would point to anything of the kind; true, the whole thing seems meaningless yet in its own way complete. … Can he die? Everything that dies has previously had some sort of goal, some kind of activity and that activity is what has worn it down; this does not apply to Odradek. And so, can I expect that one day, with his bits of thread trailing behind him, he will come clattering down the stairs, say, at the feet of my children and my grandchildren? True, he clearly harms no one; but the idea that, on top of everything else, he might outlive me, that idea I find almost painful.[8]

Although Agamben nowhere directly links Odradek to his concept of bare life, Vatter sees a close connection between the two. According to him, Odradek is the key to understanding how 'bare life that is completely subjected to sovereign power can nevertheless be the form in which human subjectivity can escape from the captivity of the law'.[9] To understand this connection, we need to look closer at Agamben's reference to Odradek. One section of Agamben's *Stanzas,* which was published almost 20 years before *Homo Sacer*, is called 'In Odradek's World'. Odradek is hardly mentioned in that section (or in the rest of the book) and the reference to Odradek does

[7] Kevin Nolan, 'Getting Past Odradek'. In *Contemporary Poetics*, edited by Louis Armand, 41–57 (Evanston: Northwestern University Press, 2007), 45.

[8] Kafka, *Selected Stories*, 72–3.

[9] Vatter, *In Odradek's World*, 46.

not seem to speak for itself, but contains an important link with the concept of bare life. In 'In Odradek's World', Agamben discusses the question of commodity fetishism, i.e. a fetishism for trade goods, that he borrows from, among others, Benjamin.

Benjamin defines the fetishism of commodities as the situation in which individuals are captivated by things that have lost their practical value and only have trade value. Things are no longer enjoyed but retained only for their market value. But, according to Benjamin, this situation contains its inversion within itself, the commodity fetishism:

> The key to this reversal is to understand that things are not destined to be simply the means through which human beings reproduce their lives. ... [C]ommodity fetishism shows that things have the potential to enjoy a life beyond that assigned by their use- and exchange-values.[10]

According to Vatter, if one wants to understand Agamben's text on Odradek, it is essential to look at Adorno's commentary on Benjamin. In a letter in which Adorno responded to Benjamin's text, he applies his friend's analysis of commodity fetishism to Odradek. He holds that Odradek is a commodity that has survived its purpose, its practical value; Odradek is an example of commodity fetishism. While Adorno views this as a matter of concern, an imperfect nihilism, an example of how things exist in capitalism (used up, forgotten, abandoned, appealing in vain to our concern), he also sees it as possibility for hope, for inversion. And this is precisely the dimension that Agamben emphasizes in his interpretation of Odradek: a possibility for a perfect nihilism, for a commodity fetishism. In Odradek's world, nothing has a place of its own; each object has lost any relation to functionality and instrumentality.[11]

In an earlier essay, Benjamin claimed that Odradek was the form things assume once they have been forgotten. He pointed out that Odradek hangs around in the same places as those where, in Kafka's work, justice carries out its investigations: in cellars, stairwells, corridors and hallways. At the same time, these places are also places where objects that have been thrown away

[10] Ibid., 51.

[11] Vatter criticizes Agamben's interpretation of Benjamin's nihilism and messianism. According to him, Agamben directs his interpretation too much towards the question of the law (p. 63). However, as we saw in the previous chapter, Agamben's interpretation of Benjamin is broader. Moreover, it is unclear whether Vatter has considered an important essay, i.e. 'The Messiah and the Sovereign', which sheds a different light on Agamben's interpretation. That notwithstanding, Vatter's criticism is in line with that voiced by others (such as Liska and Alves in 'The Messiah before the Law' and 'Diante De La Lei', respectively) who find that Agamben gives an incorrect and too radical interpretation of Benjamin.

and forgotten are found.[12] This emphasizes again the relation between law, bare life and perfect nihilism in the figure of Odradek.

In *The End of the Poem* (1996/1999), Agamben takes up the figure of Odradek again as the inversion of an imperfect nihilism or the imperfect bare life. In this book, he argues for a 'poetic atheology' in which a perfect nihilism coincides with poetic praxis and there is room for new beings like Nietzsche's Dionysius and Kafka's Odradek, beings that elude transcendence and metaphysics (EP, 64),[13] creatures that elude having a work of their own, an origin and a purpose.

The being without work of the assistants and messengers

Other examples of creatures without work in Kafka's prose are the assistants and messengers. In Kafka's works, functionaries are constantly without work. In *The Castle*, the morning after his arrival in the village at the foot of the mountain, K. sees two men approaching from the direction of the castle who look very much alike. They march in step with each other and make a cheerful impression. K. wishes they would take him with them. 'Though he did not consider this acquaintanceship all that rewarding, they were good travelling companions and could cheer one up.'[14] When he arrives at the inn somewhat later, the same two men are standing on opposite sides of the door. When K. asks who they are, they answer: 'Your assistants.' But it turns out that these assistants, Artur and Jeremias, know nothing about land surveying and the favourable impression that K. first had of them quickly fades.

Agamben remarks that 'help seems to be the last thing they are able to give. They have no knowledge, no skills and no "equipment"; they never do anything but engage in foolish behaviour and childish games; they are "pests" and sometimes "cheeky" and "lecherous"' (P, 29). It is unclear who hired them. 'They could just as easily have fallen like snowflakes, given how little thought went into assigning them.'[15] But it is not easy to get rid of them. When K. attempts to fire them, they whine: '"Let us come back to you, sir,"

[12] Benjamin, *Selected Writings 2.2*, 811.

[13] Although Agamben does not refer to it anywhere, Kafka's story 'A Crossbreed' shows a strong affinity with the above themes. This story concerns a legacy that is half lamb and half cat. The narrator does not succeed in being unequivocal about the identity of the animal: is it more lamb or more cat? Then again, it also has something of a dog about it and at the same time something human. And just as is the case with Odradek, this creature also has something immortal about it; the narrator has inherited it from his father and does not know how long it will live after he dies.

[14] Kafka, *The Castle*,14.

[15] Ibid., 62.

they cried, as if K. were the land and they were about to sink in the floods.'[16] K. tries to ignore their presence as much as possible. The messenger in *The Castle*, Barnabas, does not seem to have very much awareness of his job as a messenger either, or of the content of the letters entrusted to him. Although he looks, laughs and walks like a messenger, he himself does not seem to be conscious of that (PO, 140).

The question that arises with respect to the uselessness of the assistants and the messenger is whom they actually help. Agamben gives three answers to this that at first seem contradictory, but turn out to be complementary: their lack of work helps the 'enemy' or the sovereign power; the assistants' lack of work helps us; the assistants' lack of work helps themselves.

The first answer is that perhaps the assistants have been sent by the enemy, which would explain why they pass the time watching and spying (P, 29). At one point, K. calls to the landlady, 'Those are my assistants, but you treat them as if they were your assistants and my warders.'[17] But Agamben does not find the explanation that they are simply assistants of the 'enemy' satisfactory and this leads to the following question: *Who actually needs assistance?* We will return to this in Chapter 6.[18]

The second answer is that they actually help us through their lack of work. Everyone has friends, Agamben states, who are incomplete, who at one and the same time are divine geniuses and childish and foolish. There is always someone in one's circle of friends who is more intelligent and talented than one's other friends but nevertheless fails to finish anything. These people represent the eternal student or the swindler who ages badly. And there is something about them – an unclear gesture, an unexpected graciousness, a certain speed in their gestures or words. All these qualities allude to a lost citizenship or to a privileged elsewhere and point to the fact that such people belong to a complementary world. In that sense, they assist us, even though we cannot say what kind of assistance it is they lend us. It could consist in the fact that they cannot be helped or in 'their stubborn insistence that "there is nothing to be done for us"' (P, 30).

> But they look like angels, messengers who do not know the content of the letters they must deliver, but whose smile, whose look, whose very posture 'seems like a message'. (P, 29)

The third and perhaps most important role played by the assistants' lack of work is thus not that they assist us or the enemy, but that they belong to an intermediate world. And it is in that sense that they assist us or help

[16] Ibid., 134.

[17] Ibid., 52.

[18] Agamben argues that Kafka's point is that it is not K. who must be assisted or saved but the sovereign power itself: Klamm, the Count and anonymous crowd of guards (IP, 85).

us. The world to which the assistants belong is simultaneously unfinished and everyday, both comforting and silly.[19] Their assistance also belongs to that intermediate world and Benjamin notes that this world does not seem intended for people.[20] Precisely in this intermediate world lies an important possibility.

If Kafka claims that 'there is hope, but not for us', whom is that hope then intended for? According to Benjamin, this hope refers to the assistants, a category of extremely remarkable figures in Kafka's work. 'It is for them and their kind, the unfinished and the hapless, that there is hope.'[21] In this line of thinking, it is the assistants who are saved because they simply are 'being-thus' in their state of incompletion. In that sense, their lack of work helps them. And by showing their lack of work, as representatives of the intermediate world, the assistants bring salvation for both Joseph K. and Klamm, the Count, the judges, lawyers and guards. The assistants' lack of work coheres with the dismantling of both the higher powers and the profane power, of both the oppressed and the oppressors. This is often connected with the theme of the law that is no longer applied but only studied, as we see in Bucephalus' browsing through the books of law. Bucephalus' use of law also belongs to an intermediate world.

The irreparability of the assistants

The 'remnant' as a theological-messianic concept

The assistants' lack of work reveals a much more fundamental loss than just the loss of work. According to Agamben, 'What is lost demands not to be remembered and fulfilled but to remain forgotten or lost and therefore, for that reason alone, unforgettable' (P, 35). In Agamben's view, the assistants represent what has been lost or, better, our relation to what has been lost. The assistants are our unfulfilled desires that we do not even detect in ourselves. They prepare the Kingdom, the coming of the Messiah; on the Day of Judgement they will, like Artur and Jeremias, walk toward us laughing.

What does Agamben mean by unfulfillable and unforgettable? These terms are closely related to his concept of 'remnant'. The *polis*, the political community, attempts to create a community out of individuals. To this end it tries to find a property that all its members share and tries to identify

[19] Benjamin, *Selected Writings 2.2*, 799.
[20] Benjamin and Scholem, *Correspondence*, 327.
[21] Benjamin, *Selected Writings 2.2*, 799.

and classify them. But there is always something in the parts that does not converge with the whole. This remnant is what is left over after all dialectical attempts at exhaustive identification and classification, after all attempts to create a community that classifies the particularity of its members, have been made.[22] This remnant is often the result of (inclusive) exclusion in the *polis*. The remnant is thus the impossibility of the individual to converge completely with the community; it is the impossibility of the part and the whole to converge with each other (MWE, 29–36).

Secondly, the remnant is also the impossibility of the subject to converge completely with himself, 'something like a remnant between every people and itself, between every identity and itself' (TR, 52). This is also an opportunity to escape the sovereign power. For Agamben, the remnant is a theological-messianic concept closely associated with redemption. But if our unfulfilled desires – that in which we do not converge with ourselves – are fulfilled anyway, we are again included within the sovereign power, we are still classified and totalized. The gestures of the assistants remind us that we do not coincide with ourselves, that we are unfinished, that there is always a remnant and that this remnant is 'the little door through which the Messiah enters'. That this unfulfillment should stay unfulfilled allows us not to be totalized.

> The only possible meaning of Kafka's aphorism, in which there is salvation but 'not for us,' is found here. As remnant, we, the living who remain *en to nyn kairo*, make salvation possible, we are its 'premise' (*aparche*; Rom. 11.16). We are already saved, so to speak, but for this reason, it is not as a remnant that we will be saved. The messianic remnant exceeds the eschatological all and irremediably so; it is the unredeemable that makes salvation possible. (TR, 56–7)

In *Profanations*, Agamben gives a somewhat different interpretation of Kafka's aphorism. In this work, the relation to the lack of work, to inactivity, is central. Agamben states that Kafka's aphorism that 'there is hope but not for us' is not to say that there is hope only for others. Rather, this hope is explicitly for us, but 'it awaits only at the point where it was not destined for us'. We have not attained it by working hard or by having earned it. Agamben draws a parallel with love: how terrible it would be to be loved by a woman because one 'deserves' it. There is only one way to attain happiness, according to Agamben, i.e. 'to believe in the divine and not to aspire to reach it'. Hope and happiness need to be independent of a specific work whose goal is to

[22] DelaDurantaye, *Agamben*, 298–302.

attain such hope and happiness (P, 21–2). Happiness often has a certain arbitrariness about it.

Lack of work invokes associations with repair, with saving a specific work of man. But for Agamben, this lack of work is fundamental. But how can the unsavable make salvation possible? What does the salvation consist of if nothing can be 'repaired'?

The irreparable being-thus of things

We now return to Scholem's parable – described in Chapter 1 – where he sketches the coming world as a world in which everything is exactly the same, 'just a little different'. Scholem's friend and philosopher Ernst Bloch provided his own version of this parable: 'A rabbi, a real cabalist, once said that in order to establish the reign of peace it is not necessary to destroy everything nor to begin a completely new world. It is sufficient to displace this cup or this bush or this stone just a little and thus everything' (cited in CC, 52).

For Agamben, the paradox 'everything is the same, just a little different' sums up precisely what the messianic gesture that will bring redemption is. It is not a radical change and even less an incurable 'so be it; that's just how it is'. It is a small change that both alters and leaves everything intact. The small change here is not so much a matter of the actual circumstances changing in the sense that the cup on the table will be moved exactly one inch. This small change has more to do with the meaning and limits of things than it does with their state. The small change does not occur in the things themselves but in their thresholds, in the intimate space between each thing and itself (CC, 53). 'What changes are not the things but their limits' (CC, 91).

> We can have hope only in what is without remedy. That things are thus and thus-this is still in the world. But that this is irreparable, that this thus is without remedy, that we can contemplate it as such this is the only passage outside the world. (The innermost character of salvation is that we are saved only at the point when we no longer want to be. At this point, there is salvation – but not for us.) (CC, 101)

Benjamin sums up messianic redemption nicely as follows: 'Salvation is not a premium on existence, but the last way out for a man whose path, as Kafka puts it in "Er" [He], is "blocked ... by his own frontal bone"'.[23] Here he

[23] Here he is referring to Kafka's text in 'He': 'The bony structure of his own forehead blocks his way; he batters himself bloody against his own forehead' (Benjamin, *Selected Writing 2.2*, 804; Kafka, 'He', 154).

is referring to Kafka's text in 'He': 'The bony structure of his own forehead blocks his way; he batters himself bloody against his own forehead'. Salvation is not a remedy or repair, but a radical being-thus. When there is no way out for us, when we are blocked by our own existence, then salvation can occur in radical immanence.

What this 'little change' means is that things are still the same but they are now accepted by us in their being-thus, in their being as they are. This does not mean so much that we accept misery as that we are accepted in our being-thus. It means that we are redeemed from the distinctions that politics introduces between men and women, adults and children, people and animals, body and spirit, native and foreign, legal and illegal and all the consequences of such distinctions. It means that we are only as we are and as such 'irreparable'.

> Irreparably, but precisely this will be its novelty. … Irreparable means that these things are consigned without remedy to their being-thus, that they are precisely and only their *thus* … but irreparable also means that for them there is literally no shelter possible, that in their being-thus they are absolutely exposed, absolutely abandoned. (CC, 38)

Here we find again an inversion and a close interweaving of an aporia and a euporia, a catastrophe and a possibility. Against the imperfect nihilism of bare life, Agamben places a perfect nihilism of bare life: 'happy life might be characterized as life lived in the experience of its own unity, its own potentiality of "being-thus," and as such, is life lived beyond the reach of the law.'[24]

In *Nudities*, Agamben gives an extended explanation of what it is that is saved and links this explicitly to work. What is saved is neither the created being, nor the potentiality because the potentiality only consists of the decreation of the work.

> 'The created being and the potentiality now enter into a threshold in which they can no longer be in any way distinguished from one another. … This coincidence can be achieved only if the prophet has nothing to save and the angel has nothing else to do. Unsavable, therefore, is that work in which creation and salvation, action and contemplation, operation and inoperativity [*inoperosità*] persist in every moment and, without leaving any residue, in the same being (and in the same nonbeing).' (N, 8)

So far, different figures in Kafka's prose that showed a being without work, a radical being-thus, have been described. The specific kind of help the

[24] Mills, *Agamben's Messianic Politics*, 49.

assistants offer in showing this form of life to us, this hope that only appears when it is no longer for us, is explained. Agamben acknowledges that this demands quite a shift in the way we think about salvation and that not everyone is glad with this salvation. An example of this can be found in his story of Sancho Panza's saving of Dulcinea.

Sancho Panza's saving of Dulcinea

Although Agamben nowhere provides a direct interpretation of Kafka's story 'The Truth about Sancho Panza', he does refer to it indirectly in *Profanations*, in the form of his own version of the story. He uses this story as an example of what the salvation of society looks like, what the salvation of the irreparable being-thus looks like.

Kafka's version of the original story of Don Quixote written by Cervantes appeared in Agamben's work via an interpretation by Benjamin.[25] Cervantes' story is about a man who is obsessed by stories about knights and decides to knight himself as Don Quixote and to go on various quests. He persuades a certain Sancho Panza to accompany him as his squire and declares Dulcinea to be his princess. He thus starts out on numerous unsuccessful adventures and it is usually Sancho Panza who ends up paying the price for these.

In his 'The Truth about Sancho Panza', Kafka gives the following version of this story in which Sancho Panza is not so much the victim as the one that is one step ahead:

> Without making any boast of it Sancho Panza succeeded in the course of years, by feeding him a great number of romances of chivalry and adventure in the evening and night hours, in so diverting from himself his demon, whom he later called Don Quixote, that this demon thereupon set out, uninhibited, on the maddest exploits, which, however, for the lack of a preordained object, which should have been Sancho Panza himself, harmed nobody. A free man, Sancho Panza philosophically followed Don Quixote on his crusades, perhaps out of a sense of responsibility and had of them a great and edifying entertainment to the end of his days.[26]

25 In his article 'Going Along for the Ride. Violence and Gesture. Agamben Reading Benjamin Reading Kafka Reading Cervantes,' Weber (2006) explores the complex relationship between Agamben and Benjamin in their interpretation of Kafka. Although Agamben seems to follow Benjamin in many cases, he often takes his interpretation one step further.

26 Franz Kafka, *The Complete Stories*, trans. N. Glatzer (New York: Schocken Books, 1995), 430.

Benjamin has great admiration for the inversion in this story: Sancho Panza succeeds in letting his demon precede him so that the burden is lifted from his shoulders and he can follow him like a free man.[27]

Agamben provides his own interpretation of this parable in the form of a story of another unsuccessful adventure of Don Quixote, which does not make only Don Quixote harmless, but also the whole metaphysical politics. He does this by showing the metaphysical structure laid upon the world, hoping this gesture will save the princess Dulcinea. Agamben's story goes as follows. One night Sancho Panza goes to a cinema, looking for Don Quixote. He cannot get to him because the cinema is full and sits down next to a girl, probably Dulcinea, who offers him a lollipop. The film begins, but as soon as the main character of the film is in trouble, Don Quixote jumps up to save her. He draws his sword and cuts the screen to ribbons, leaving only the wooden frame behind. Furious, the adults in the cinema leave, but the children cheer Don Quixote. Only Dulcinea looks at him with disapproval.

Agamben states that Don Quixote, who is always obsessed with saving Dulcinea, shows to the enchanted movie watchers that the movie, their world, is only a wooden frame. Only the children approve of the world's being-thus and the salvation it offers, but Dulcinea is disappointed. Agamben asks: What do we do with our illusions? We want to love them and to believe in them, but there comes a point when we can only destroy them and then we see what they cost: the person we have saved, Dulcinea, cannot love us (P, 94).

Liska views this as a parallel with Agamben's own work and the salvation he offers, which is not seen by his critics as salvation but as the unveiling of the structure of the world as a lamentable wooden frame. She argues that Agamben has entertained us in a grand and profitable way, but he has not relieved the world of its burden.[28] For Agamben this is exactly the most perfect salvation and he calls this the six most beautiful minutes in the history of cinema. In these six minutes the structure of the world is revealed to be a wooden frame, in which it is revealed that the one whom we have saved cannot love us, in which it does not matter, perhaps, that the one whom we have saved cannot love us (P, 94).[29]

In her recapitulation of the content of Kafka's letters that the Gestapo took and that are considered lost, Dora Dymant describes how Kafka was

[27] Benjamin, *Selected Writings 2.2*, 816.

[28] Vivian Liska, 'The Messiah before the Law', 174.

[29] Weber points out that while Benjamin sees an inversion between Sancho Panza and Don Quixote, in Agamben the distinction between Sancho Panza and Don Quixote disappears when he states that 'the one whom *we* have saved cannot love us.' In this sentence, the reader, writer, Don Quixote and Sancho Panza merge into one.

preoccupied with the question of Tolstoy's fight for his own liberation and that Kafka mentioned that he found some '"technical errors" in the way man acts towards himself'[30]. We will perhaps never know what Kafka meant by this, but it may refer to our expectations of our 'work' and our 'salvation'.

[30] Hodin, 'Kafka', 43.

5

Strategies in Response to Activism

Kafka could understand things only in the form of a gestus.

(Walter Benjamin)[1]

Introduction

What other strategy do creatures without work have beyond being-thus? If there is no specific 'work' or task for them, what does their 'activity' look like? How are we to 'do' nothing? Or is resistance without 'activity' possible? Is the question 'What do we have to do?' the right question to ask? Or does this question only reflect the compulsion of metaphysics, the desire for activism, for a task, for an activity that realizes a potential? How is being-thus related to the abolishment of a subject and an activity ascribed to that subject? In the same way that the subject cannot be a bearer of resistance, active, goal-directed, planned actions are not an effective response to power and even, perhaps, maintain power. These themes will be discussed in the first section, 'the Compulsion of Activism'. In the following sections, three strategies against the drive of activism will be described.

An answer to the question 'What do we have to do?' can be found in the theatrical gestures often present in Kafka's works and in his fascination with theatre. How can a gesture be a form of resistance? And how is it related to being-thus and to the metaphysical attempts to turn the human being into a subject and to attribute deliberate action to it?

Two examples of gestures as a form of resistance that Agamben reads in Kafka's work will be discussed: Joseph K.'s shame and the 'as not' in 'On Parables'. What is the role of Joseph K.'s shame when he dies? What light does this throw on the relation between passivity and activity, between being subjected and being a subject? Kafka's enigmatic 'On Parables' shows a similar gesture: the acting 'as not' that abolishes every claim of specific activity or properties allocated to the subject.

[1] Benjamin, *Selected Writings 2.2*, 808

The compulsion of activism

Given the preceding sketch Agamben gives of power and possibilities (the law's being in force without significance, the subtle reverse found in Kafka's work of this situation, Agamben's praise of creatures without work), the questions arise: what ought we to do now? What form of resistance is possible for us? How should we act? What can we do? This is actually one of the major criticisms on Agamben's work, that in it, at least when read superficially, Agamben nowhere seems to formulate any explicit answer to the question of resistance.

The Italian political philosopher Antonio Negri, also one of Agamben's close friends, points out that Agamben was never directly involved in political struggles and he sees this as a great lack in his philosophy.[2] Agamben's work is often described as a radical passivity.[3] This passivity can be seen both as a strength and a weakness of his work. Agamben's passivity is not a regular powerlessness, but seems to come close to (Mahayana) Buddhism, an exercise in doing nothing.[4] This passivity also shows evidence of a radical paradigm shift in thinking about power and resistance, a movement that is often attributed to Foucault and whose traces can be found in Kafka *avant la lettre*. As is evident from the above, Agamben is fundamentally opposed to the tendency of metaphysical politics to attribute an identity to the human being, to allocate to him a work of his own. If the human being has no identity of his own and no activity of his own, then this also has consequences for our traditional view of actions as being fundamentally embedded within end-means relationships, as goal-oriented in essence. Our views of activities and activism must therefore be thoroughly revised in line with our revision of the possibility of a transcendent work of man.

Kafka's opera singing executioners or questioners

Deleuze once defined power as the act in which the human being is cut off from its potentiality. But, Agamben states, 'There is, nevertheless, another

[2] Antonio Negri and Cesare Casarino. 'It's a Powerful Life: A Conversation on Contemporary Philosophy'. *Cultural Critique 57*, no. Spring (2004), 171.

[3] Thomas Carl Wall. Radical Passivity: Lévinas, Blanchot and Agamben (New York: State University of New York Press, 1999).

[4] See, for example, Agamben's reference to Nagarjuna in *Idea of Prose* ('The Idea of Awakening', p.131). Mahayana Buddhism sees Nagarjuna, the founder of the still influential Madhyamaka school, as perhaps the greatest master of all – after the Buddha himself. This is the only explicit reference by Agamben to Buddhism, although many of his concepts, such as radical passivity and 'doing nothing', being-thus, have a strong Buddhist, as well as Taoist, air about them. See, e.g. *The Coming Community*. My thanks to Gijsbert van der Heijden for pointing this out to me.

and more insidious operation of power that does not immediately affect what humans can do – their potentiality – but rather their "impotentiality", that is, what they cannot do, or better, can *not do*' (N, 43). Given that flexibility is the primary quality the market requires from us, the contemporary human, yielding to every demand by society, is cut off from his impotentiality, from his ability to do nothing. Just as we saw previously, politics is a politics of the act, of the human individual being at work. The irresponsible motto of the contemporary individual, 'No problem, I can do it', comes precisely at the moment 'when he should instead realize that he has been consigned in unheard of measure to forces and processes over which he has lost all control' (N, 44).

This flexibility also leads to a confusion of professions and callings, of professional identities and social roles, because people are no longer in touch with their inability. Agamben sees an example of this in Kafka's *The Trial*. In the last chapter, just before his death, two men enter through Joseph K.'s door. They are his questioners/executioners, but Joseph K. does not recognize them as such and thinks that they are '[o]ld second-rate actors or opera singers?'[5]

Agamben argues that, in Kafka's world, evil is presented as an inadequate reaction to impotentiality (CC, 31). Instead of making use of our possibility of 'not being', we fail it, we flee from our lack of power, 'our fearful retreat from it in order to exercise … some power of being' (CC, 32). But this power we try to exercise turns into a malevolent power that oppresses the persons who show us their weakness. In Kafka's world, evil does not have the form of the demonic but that of being separated from our lack of power.

> Nothing makes us more impoverished and less free than this estrangement from impotentiality. Those who are separated from what they can do, can, however, still resist; they can still not do. Those who are separated from their own impotentiality lose, on the other hand, first of all the capacity to resist. (N, 45)

And it is evident, according to Agamben, from the example of Eichmann how right Kafka was in this (CC, 32). Eichmann was not so much separated from his power as from his lack of power, tempted to evil precisely by the powers of right and law (CC, 32).

What should one do? A clash with activists

At the end of 2009, Agamben gave a lecture in honour of the presentation of a collection of texts written by the Tiqqun collective. This French collective

[5] Kafka, *The Trial*, 161.

has written several political manifestoes and in 2008 their compound was raided by the anti-terrorist brigades. The charges were quite vague: belonging to an ultra-left and the anarcho-autonomous milieu; using a radical discourse; having links with foreign groups; participating regularly in political demonstrations. The evidence that was found was not weapons, but documents, for example a train schedule.

Although Agamben calls these charges a tragicomedy and accuses French politics of barbarism[6], in his lecture he emphasizes another important political value of the Tiqqun collective. This collective embodies Foucault's idea of the non-subject. One of the latter's greatest merits is that he thought of power no longer as an attribute that a certain group had over another, but as a relation that was constantly shifting. A second merit of Foucault's thinking was the idea of non-authorship. The subject itself, its identity, is always formed within a power relation, a process that Foucault termed 'subjectivization techniques'.

In Foucault, the state attempts to form the subject via disciplinary techniques and the subject responds via subjectivization techniques: it internalizes the expectations of the state in the formation of its own identity. That is why Foucault rejects the idea of a subject and the idea of actorship, of attributing an act to a subject. Hence, as long as we continue to think in terms of a subject resisting oppressive power via deliberate action, we cannot liberate ourselves from power relations. The gesture Tiqqun instead is making is, according to Agamben, not one of looking for a subject that can assume the role of saviour or revolutionary. Rather, they begin with investigating the force fields that are operative in our society (instead of focusing on the subject). In describing these fields of force and the moment they become diffuse, new possibilities can arise that are not dependent on a subject.

The discussion that followed this lecture provides a very clear picture of Agamben's position. Many activists present at the lecture asked what his theory entailed concretely with respect to the direction in which they should go. Agamben's constant reply was that anyone who poses this question has not understood the problem at all.

> I always find it out of place to go and ask someone what to do, what is there to be done? … If someone asks me what action, it shows they missed the point because they still want me to say: go out in the streets and do this? It has nothing to do with that. (OT)

Inactivity as active resistance to the state was hardly conceivable for many of the left wing activists present at Agamben's lecture at Tiqqun. Although

[6] Giorgio Agamben. 'Terrorism or Tragicomedy'. *Libération* November 19, (2008).

the state acknowledges the anti-law tendencies in the writings of the Tiqqun collective, the activists present at Agamben's lecture failed to recognize this specific form of resistance. What Agamben attempted to show was that the power of the Tiqqun collective lay precisely in the fact that they did not prescribe any concrete actions but sought unexpected possibilities in 'being-thus'. In that same sense, Agamben's analysis of Kafka's work should not be seen as a manual for activist freedom but as a description of small opportunities, of examples in which the power relation is diffuse and that we must attempt to recognize, create and use.

Agamben shows us different possibilities and means for resistance, but these are not regular acts with a goal; rather, they are means without end. As Kishik pointed out, Agamben's work is an attempt to '"make means meet" (not with their ends, but with each other)'.[7] One way to achieve this is through gestures. The gestures of the people in the Oklahoma theatre and elsewhere in Kafka's work, the shame of Joseph K. and the 'as not' in Kafka's 'On Parables' show us that there are other strategies, aside from active resistance, to reverse political situations.

The gestures of the Oklahoma theatre

A group of Yiddish actors came to Prague late in 1911. Although, according to Kafka biographer Pawel, they did not do well and received bad reviews, these eight players made a deep impression on Kafka. He went to about 20 performances in half a year's time, became friends with the organiser and star of the company, Jizschak Löwy and fell in love with another member, Mania Tschissik. His journal entries testify to a great enthusiasm for this theatre company. Pawel argues that there is thus reason enough to conclude that seeing these performances had a permanent influence on his work and his whole development.[8] The American professor of comparative literature, Evelyn Torton Beck, devoted a complete monograph to this, *Kafka and the Yiddish Theater: Its Impact on His Work*.[9] Beck points out that 1912, the year in which Kafka wrote *The Trial*, is seen as his breakthrough year. In her view, it is not a coincidence that this was also the period in which Kafka became acquainted with the Yiddish theatre and his work acquired theatrical

[7] Kishik, *Power of Life*, 49.
[8] Pawel, *Nightmare of Reason*, 274–5.
[9] Evelyn Beck, *Kafka and the Yiddish Theater. Its Impact on His Work* (Madison, Milwaukee and London: The University of Wisconsin Press, 1971).

characteristics. Kafka's stories seem to be written from the perspective of a visitor to the theatre.[10]

But what was it about the theatre that interested him primarily? Kafka's journal entries on his impressions of Yiddish theatre show an obsession with gestures.[11] Walter Benjamin was one of the first to remark that the gestures of Kafka's main characters are often 'too powerful for our accustomed surroundings and break out into wider areas'.[12] Thus, the villagers in the courtyard village, who hear the knock on the courtyard gate, are 'cowering in terror'. Only an actor would portray fear in that way, Benjamin claims; no one really cowers in fear.[13] In *The Trial*, K. 'stopped beside the front pews, but the distance still seemed too great for the priest. He stretched out his arm and indicated, his forefinger pointing sharply downward, a place just in front of the pulpit. K. obeyed him in this as well, from that spot he had to bend his head right back to see the priest'.[14] Elsewhere, K. acts deliberately and intentionally in a theatrical way. 'Slowly, … with his eyes not looking down but cautiously raised upward, he took one of the papers from the desk, put it on the palm of his hand and gradually raised it up to the gentlemen while getting up himself. He had nothing definite in mind'.[15] Another example of theatrical gesturality in Kafka's work is the new lawyer who '[l]ifting his thighs high, mounted step by step with a stride that made the marble clang'.[16] According to Benjamin, these emphatic gestures are of essential importance in Kafka's work: 'Kafka could understand things only in the form of a *gestus*.'[17]

For Benjamin, the nature theatre of Oklahoma refers to a theatre of gesture, that is, a theatre in which the action is absorbed into gestures. Each gesture is an event – one could even say, a play in itself. Kafka's world is a theatre of the world: the human being is on stage as such.[18] Kafka's work can be said to form a code of gestures that he continues to try out in different contexts and experimental groupings and the theatre is the logical place for that.

Although Benjamin points, on the one hand, to the importance of gestures in Kafka's work, he emphasizes on the other that in no way did these gestures have a fixed symbolic meaning for Kafka. He describes these

[10] Ibid., 5.
[11] Sternstein, 'Laughter, Gesture and Flesh', 317.
[12] Benjamin, *Selected Writings 2.2*, 801.
[13] Ibid., 802.
[14] Kafka, *Trial*, 151.
[15] Kafka, cited in: Benjamin *Selected Writings 2.2*, 801.
[16] Kafka, *Selected Stories*, 60.
[17] Benjamin, *Selected Writings 2.2*, 808.
[18] Ibid., 800–2.

gestures as 'cloudy' places in Kafka's work.[19] They make Kafka's work both naturalistic as well as very difficult to interpret.[20]

The structure of the gesture as resistance

Benjamin's conclusion that the gestures in Kafka, despite their essential function, do not have any fixed meaning can only be better understood if we explore the structure of the gesture more closely. Three things are important here: the role of the body, the relation between means and end and the extent to which a gesture is deliberately made by an actor.

The first characteristic of the gesture is that physicality plays a major role. A gesture is not so much a cognitively planned action as it is a physical event, a physical expression. This physicality of gestures is displayed in various ways in Kafka. The scenes are almost always public and the arms, legs, eyes, ears and hair of his characters seem to lead lives of their own, a life at least as complex as the characters' mental lives and thoughts.[21] That gestures have their location in the body also explains Kafka's emphasis on torture, nakedness, death and the physical ability to suffer pain, as emerges in, for example, 'In the Penal Colony' and 'A Country Doctor'. In 'A Country Doctor', Kafka describes the worms in a wound 'as thick and as long as my little finger, rose-pink themselves and also blood-spattered, firmly attached to the inside of the wound'.[22] That the body plays a central role in the gesture means that physical vulnerability does so as well. A gesture places one's life at stake 'irrevocably and without reserve – even at the risk that its happiness or its disgrace will be decided once and for all' (P, 69).

The second characteristic of the gesture is the specific relation between means and end in the gesture. In *Ethica Nicomachea*, Aristotle distinguishes between actions that have an end beyond themselves (*poiesis*), such as walking to the bakery and actions that are ends in themselves (*praxis*), such as dancing.

The Latin writer Varro elaborates on this distinction and adds a third type of action. Whilst establishing a relation akin to the distinction between *poiesis* and *praxis* – *facere*, making, from *agere*, doing – he introduces still a third type of action: *gerere* (gesturing), in which nothing is being made or done but only undergone. This undergoing is not only passive, but also remains active in a certain sense. It is distinguished from actions that are

[19] Ibid., 801.
[20] Sternstein, 'Laughter, Gesture and Flesh', 317.
[21] Ibid., 318.
[22] Ibid., 320; Kafka, *Selected Stories*, 63.

means to ends and actions that are ends in themselves. This third type of action is a means without an end, pure mediality (MWE, 55). Werner Hamacher defines it as 'non-action in action'.[23] Looking at Kafka's gestures, it is difficult to point to their ends, even though they do have a function. 'Gesture is the decisive thing because in it nothing happens but itself; the distinction between playing and being is, for gesture, just as pointless as the distinction between meaning and the object meant.'[24] A gesture is a means without an end (IH, MWE).[25] Form and content converge completely in the gesture and this reminds us of Agamben's concept of being-thus: in a gesture the body is 'shown' beyond subjectivity. This brings us to the relationship between the gesture and the author.

The third characteristic is that gestures do not have an explicit author. Gestures are movements of the human being that are not planned actions, or that one does without exactly knowing why one does them; they have a certain spontaneity. Mills uses the examples of tics, such as wiggling one's foot, stroking one's chin or nose, pressing one's lips together or playing with one's hair. Although these gestures can be seen as indications of concentration, surprise or boredom, they are not intended as such: they are done without an end, often without one being aware they are being done.[26] This is perhaps why gesture is not, or not in the first place, action or act, but something remaining once action or act have carved up and articulated the world in terms of means and ends. Thus Kafka writes in *The Blue Octavo Notebooks:* it is not an act but an event.[27] Just as it cancels the relation between means and end, so gesture also interrupts the relation between actor and act. And perhaps in gesture the strict dividing line between human and animal is canceled as well. Agamben quotes Kommerell, who speaks of a new beauty, 'one that is similar to the beauty of the gestures of an animal, to soft and threatening gestures' (PO, 80).

An example of a gesture is the student who faced down a tank on Tiananmen Square. He had no clear goal, he did not shout any slogans, he simply stood there alone in front of the tank. Physically he could never have stopped a tank, so his act had a different meaning. And this gesture confused the political power. This image, which travelled over the whole world, is

[23] Werner Hamacher, 'The Gesture in the Name: On Benjamin and Kafka'. In *Premises: Essays on Philosophy and Literature from Kant to Celan* (Stanford, CA: Stanford University Press, 1999), 333.

[24] Ibid., 331.

[25] René Ten Bos, 'On the Possibility of Formless Life: Agamben's Politics of the Gesture'. *Ephemera. theory & politics in organization* 5, no. 1 (2005): 26–44.

[26] Mills, *The Philosophy of Agamben*, 127.

[27] Kafka, *Octavo Notebooks*, 40.

somewhat more anonymous than, for example, the revolutionary icon Che Guevara. This image has no author, no proclamations.

For Agamben, gesture plays an important role in the dismantling of sovereign power. Gesture is an opportunity for life to throw sand into the cogs of the machinery of law and politics. Crucial to understanding gesture, it is important to realize that in Agamben this 'throwing sand' is gestural and hence is not at all a matter of political activism, of overthrowing power – which always threatens to become stuck in the same structure as that which it fights. Nor is it a matter of using the law or sovereign power in the right way. Rather, it is a matter of playing with the law, confusing it in a way that renders it inoperative. Kafka's work is bursting with diffuse events and gestures, gestures that make the relation between law and life inoperative. Gestures are the activity of creatures that are only being-thus. Gestures 'show' being-thus. I will give two examples below of gestures in Kafka's work: shame and acting 'as not'.

Joseph K.'s shame

Kafka as the prophet of shame

On the eve of his thirty-first birthday two men enter Joseph K.'s home. Were they '[o]ld second-rate actors or opera singers?' K. wonders, but they do not respond to his question, 'At which theatre are you engaged?'[28] They prove to be his questionees who have come to torture him. They take him to an old quarry where they stab him in the heart with a knife. And thus ends *The Trial* and the life of Joseph K.:

> As his sight faded, K. saw the two men leaning cheek to cheek close to his face as they observed the final verdict. 'Like a dog!' he said. It seemed as if his shame would live on after him.[29]

How must we understand the execution of K. and his shame at the end of *The Trial*? Is it a betrayal of the immanence that this book expresses, as Deleuze and Guattari have claimed?[30] Is it a defeat of K.? Or has it another function?

According to Agamben, Kafka has given us an immanence of shame. Kafka's genius consists in the gesture to 'renounce theodicy and forego the old problem of guilt and innocence, of freedom and destiny, in order to

[28] Kafka, *The Trial*, 161.
[29] Ibid., 165.
[30] Deleuze and Guattari, *Kafka*, 44; 88.

concentrate solely on shame' (IP, 85). Walter Benjamin claims that the shame that survives is Kafka's noblest and strongest gesture and characterizes Kafka as a prophet of shame.[31] Agamben also describes Kafka as a good prophet (RA, 104) and *The Trial* as a truly prophetic book (MWE, 122). Moran has looked closer at the relationship between prophecy, shame and dehumanizing political situations. What Kafka prophesied was not only an oppressive future, but also a potential freedom fueled by shame.[32] He portrays Kafka as a prophet of shame,[33] but what is the role of shame in this story of Kafka?

Shame: Between passivity and activity, undergoing and undertaking

At first glance, shame seems to have little to do with resistance and more with defeat, with passivity, with paralysis. But Karl Marx attributed a major role to the emotion of shame. When the Hegelian Arnold Ruge states that no single revolution ever *originated* in shame, Marx responds that shame is already a revolution *in itself* (cited in MWE, 131). Agamben, who cites Marx approvingly, points out that in ancient Greece shame was not an uncomfortable feeling. Rather, people who were confronted with their shame rediscovered their courage and compassion, as Hector did before the exposed breast of his mother Hecuba (IP, 85). Agamben sees this shame, which played such an important role in ancient Greece, returning in Kafka's work, in the mythic filth of his courts and castles (IP, 83). Thus, shame is not only a passive emotion but also includes active elements. But these elements do not need to lead to a Greek heroic act or a communist revolution. Rather, they refer to a more subtle relation to oneself, to power and most of all to ethics. According to Mills, for Agamben, 'shame is the mode by which the subject comes to ethical responsibility'.[34]

Shame: Not guilt but subjectivity

Agamben sees a special relationship between shame, subjectivity and testimony. Shame is not about guilt but about subjectivity. Agamben defines

[31] Benjamin, *Selected Writings 2.2*, 808.

[32] Moran, 'Kafka's Prophecy', 285. Moran points out that, although Benjamin and Agamben have differences in their interpretation of Kafka with regard to emphasis, terminology and historical perspective, it is an overstatement to say that Agamben's interpretation is a betrayal of that of Benjamin and that his interpretations of Kafka are a less radical departure from those of Benjamin than is usually assumed. (285; 288).

[33] Brendan Moran, 'Kafka's Prophecy, with Benjamin and Agamben'. *Philosophy Today* 55, no. Sept. supplement (2011), 288.

[34] Mills, *The Philosophy of Agamben*, 93.

shame as the impossibility of removing oneself from oneself, the impossibility of removing oneself from a particular presentation of oneself.[35]

If, for example, we are ashamed of being naked, then we are not ashamed because we feel guilt. We are ashamed because we are seen and cannot withdraw our being-thus from this gaze. We feel that we are desubjectified, we do not feel a subject, but a naked version of ourself. At the same time, not only are we seen but *we see* that we are seen. If we do not see that someone sees us naked, we would not be ashamed. We are witnesses of our own desubjectification.

> In shame, the subject thus has no other content than its own desubjectification; it becomes witness to its own disorder, its own oblivion as a subject. (RA, 106)[36]

Agamben's philosophy of subjectivity is developed in close relation with desubjectivity; subjectivity can only exist in relation to a process of desubjectivity and shame is the process that illustrates this best.

Two things are important here: first, shame is a gesture that binds people in a different way to their subjectivity. As we saw at the beginning of this book, Agamben, following Foucault, rejects the idea of a subject as the basis for a theory of freedom. The subject comes to existence in a power relation and cannot be conceived in its entirety apart from this. In shame, the subject witnesses his own desubjectification. Shame is both loss of self and being inseparably connected to oneself and thus not being able to do anything else but take possession of oneself. This shame is twofold according to Moran: shame about the decomposition of the subject and shame about the relationship between the subjectivity and the power. This last one is the type of shame that will survive.[37] But Agamben also sees a possibility in this experience of shame. Shame is nothing other than the fundamental feeling of being a subject in both opposite meanings of the word: on the one hand, we are subjected and, on the other, are sovereign, independent (RA, 107). Shame, then, is the feeling by which the human being most closely approaches himself (IP, 84).

The second important point in the above citation is the relation between shame and testimony. Shame makes testimony possible, even though it cannot be directly assigned to a specific subject. At the same time, shame is the 'dwelling place' of the subject. What survives with shame is testimony.

35 Ibid., 90.

36 Santner takes Agamben's definition here a step further. The actual paradox of shame is, according to him, that shame is aroused by the same power as that which confronts us with shame. Santner, *On Creaturely Life*, 24.

37 Moran, 'Kafka's Prophecy', 288.

So shame itself is not so much a gesture, but the testimony of shame, the testimony of Joseph K.'s shame that leaps forward to us through Kafka and Agamben. Agamben investigates the relation between shame and testimony further via testimonies from Nazi concentration camps.[38]

Shame: Ethical responsibility

One author that is especially important for Agamben's theory of shame and subjectivity is Auschwitz survivor Primo Levi. In 1983, the Italian publisher Einaudi asked the writer Primo Levi to translate Kafka's *The Trial* into Italian (RA, 18). Agamben sees a strong connection between the work of Levi and Kafka. In his memoirs, Levi describes a specific kind of shame he experienced in the camps: shame about the fact that one is human.

> The shame … that the just man experiences at another man's crime, at the fact that such a crime should exist, that it should have been introduced irrevocably into the world of things that exist and that his will for good should have proved too weak or null and should not have availed in defence.[39]

Agamben describes a similar type of shame in his journal on the political situation in Italy: the shame we feel when we are confronted with a certain vulgarity in thinking, when we watch certain TV shows, when we are confronted with the self-conscious smiles of 'experts' who cheerfully lend their expertise to the political game of the media. It is the shame we feel when Joseph K. is killed like a dog.

In this shame the fullness of gesturality is revealed, a sign of resistance, because those who suffer this shame of being human rebel against their being subjected and thus rebel against the political power under which they live. It nourishes their thoughts and forms the beginning of a revolution or

[38] Agamben's use of testimony literature from the concentration camps to support his theory of shame has been much criticized. Hutchinson reproaches Agamben for selectively quoting Levi and Antelme only for the sake of obtaining phenomenological support for his theory. Mesnard and Kahan find the comparison between Joseph K. and the witness of the Nazi concentration camps to be completely arbitrary and that the latter is of a different order. Agamben's method, however, does not propose that all shame in the concentration camps had the specific form he describes but uses a few examples of shame that can serve as a paradigm for a form of life beyond subjectivity. Anthony Hutchinson, *Shame and Philosophy: An Investigation in the Philosophy of Emotions and Ethics* (Palgrave Macmillan, 2008), 74; Philippe Mesnard and Claudine Kahan, *Giorgio Agamben À L'épreuve D'auschwitz. Temoignages/Interpretations* (Paris: Éditions Kimé, 2001), 111–12.

[39] Primo Levi, *Survival in Auschwitz and the Reawakening: Two Memoirs* (New York: Summit Books, 1986), 181–2; translation slightly modified by Agamben.

an exodus whose end is barely in sight. At the moment when the knife of his questioners penetrates his heart, Joseph K. succeeds, with a final leap, in holding on to the shame that will survive him (MWE, 132).[40] In that way, he makes a gesture, breaks the tie to political power and eludes political power. For what is Joseph K. ashamed about? His shame betrays a limit that has been reached, a new ethical dimension that has been touched in his existence. Something overcomes him and he cannot testify to that something in any other way. But his shame flies through time like a silent apostrophe to reach us, to testify for him (RA, 104).

Agamben argues that Kafka attempts to save 'at least its shame' for humankind. Our only possible innocence consists of subjecting ourselves to shame, a shame without embarrasment, a shame that lets us regain our courage and pity, as in ancient Greece. Kafka shows us how we can use this shame: not to free us from shame but to free the shame in ourselves. That is what Joseph K. attempts during the whole process. What he attempts to save is not his own innocence but his own shame (IP, 85). In this sense, *The Trial* is a prophetic book and not only with regards to the camps. It reveals a situation of political suffering that we cannot witness as subjects, but can only respond to with shame.[41]

The 'as not' of the parable 'On Parables'

A second gesture that can be found in Kafka's work is the 'as not' described in the parable 'On Parables'. According to Marthe Robert, Kafka's technique is characterized by an 'as if'.[42] In *The Trial*, K. has the feeling that he has

[40] Moran (2009) points out that Agamben interprets Kafka somewhat more radically than the source text allows, but it may very well be that both authors have given their own interpretations based on different source texts. What is stated in *The Trial* is: '*(...) as war, als sollte die Scham ihn überleben*.' This has been translated into 'It seemed as if his shame would live on after him' (trans. Breon Mitchell). Unfortunately, this translation is an approximation and it does not do justice to the German verb *sollen*. *Sollen* emphasizes a necessity (ought to, had to) and not just a possibility (would), such that the German original would justify a more radical interpretation compared to the English translation. Agamben paraphrases this to say that Joseph K. clings successfully to the shame that would survive him. The conviction with which Agamben states this is perhaps part of his trust in the fact that the driving shame about sovereign power cannot be uprooted: it is inhuman, it does not wallow in pathos and it does not have any anthropomorphic characteristics. Shame is one way to think outside the existing boxes. Brendan Moran, 'An Inhumanly Wise Shame'. *The European Legacy* 14, no. 5 (2009), 573–85.

[41] Moran, 'Kafka's Prophecy', 289.

[42] Marthe Robert, *L'ancien Et Le Nouveau : De Don Quichotte Á Kafka* (Paris: Éditions Payot, 1967); Barthes, Roland, 'Kafka's Answer'. In *Critical Essays* (Evanston: Northwestern University Press, 1972); Alan Udoff, 'Kafka's Question'. In *Kafka and the Contemporary Critical Performance* (Bloomington: Indiana University Press, 1987).

been arrested and everything occurs *as if* he has been arrested. In 'The Metamorphosis', everything happens *as if* the main character is transformed into a large insect. Håkan Gustafsson describes the law in Kafka as an 'as if'.[43] But Agamben states that Kafka's work could more accurately be described as an 'as not' (TR, 42).

Whereas the 'as if' presupposes a relation between a subject and a similitude, between an ascriber of meaning and what is meant,[44] the 'as not' (which Agamben sees as a messianic gesture) is simultaneously the abolition and the realization of the 'as if'. Agamben finds this in Kafka's parable on parables in which the subject, while contemplating his ruin, simply loses the wager through his wish to be preserved indefinitely in similitude (in the 'as if').

> Many complained that the words of the wise are over and over again merely parables, of no use in everyday life and that's all we have. When the wise man says, 'Go across', he does not mean that you ought to cross the street to the other side, something that you could manage if the result were worth the trip. But what he means is some fabulous Beyond, something we have never known, which he cannot describe more accurately and therefore can be of no help to us in this case. In effect, all these parables merely attempt to say that the inconceivable is inconceivable and we knew that already. But the matters we truly struggle with every day are different. In response, someone said, 'Why do you resist? If you'd follow the parables, you'd become parables yourselves and with that, free of the everyday struggle.' Someone else said, 'I bet that is a parable too.' The first one said, 'You win'. The second one said, 'But unfortunately only in a parable.' The first one said, 'No, in reality; in the parable you lost.'[45]

What Kafka, according to Agamben, unerringly feels and attempts to articulate in this exceptional parable is that the messianic is simultaneously the abolition and the realization of the 'as if', that is, it is an 'as not' (TR, 42). The fulfillment of the 'as if' (the following of the parables) means the end (liberation) of the representation (of the similitude). In the 'as not', subjects once and for all abolish their presupposed identity and attributes (TR, 41). In the words of Kishik:

[43] Håkan Gustafsson, '"As If": Behind before the Law.' Law and Critique 6, no. 1 (1996), 109.

[44] David Johnson, '"as If" the Time Were Now: Deconstructing Agamben'. *South Atlantic Quarterly* 106, no. 2 (2007), 273.

[45] Kafka, *Selected Stories*, 161–2.

> Since no identity is sacred, the ethical task is actually to profane it, use it, play with it, examine it, struggle for and against it, or even render it completely inoperative within our life, but without trying to resolve the matter once and for all. A whatever singularity may accept and reject the same identity or shuttle between a number of identities. Rather than being x (insert here your identity of choice), try to be and not to be x.[46]

The 'as not' is not directed towards a specific other 'being' but folds what exists back on itself out of an inherent tension with itself, without desire to coincide with itself or with something else; it is a remnant (TR, 66).

In his Letter to the Romans, St. Paul speaks of the messianic life as weeping as if one is not weeping, rejoicing as if one is not rejoicing and using the things of the world as if one is not using them (1 Cor. 7.29–32, cited in TR, 23–4). Agamben claims that this is the original messianic gesture (TR, 23–4). Benjamin describes a similar gesture in relation to Kafka's students. In describing Karl's study as an 'as not', Benjamin states: 'Perhaps these studies amounted to nothing. But if so, they stand in close proximity to that nothing, which alone makes anything useful'.[47] Benjamin quotes Kafka's wish from 'He':

> As if one were to hammer together a table with painful and methodical technical efficiency and simultaneously do nothing at all and not in such a way that people could say: 'Hammering a table together is nothing to him', but rather, 'Hammering a table together is really hammering a table together to him, but at the same time it is nothing', whereby certainly the hammering would have become still bolder, still surer, still more real and, if you will, still more senseless.[48]

Kafka's students display the same resolution and fanaticism when they are studying, according to Benjamin.[49]

To conclude, the above 'as not' is the realization and abolition of the 'as if'. The gesture is the sign of potentiality, of the irreparable, of the tension between being and not being, between act and suspension, of making power inoperative. The gesture is an 'as not' in which Agamben sees the ultimate messianic life taking form.

[46] Kishik, *Power of Life*, 83.
[47] Benjamin, *Selected Writings 2.2*, 814.
[48] Kafka, 'He', 155.
[49] Benjamin, *Selected Writings 2.2*, 814.

6

Strategies in Response to the Sacrality of Life

What changes are not the things but their limits.

(Agamben, CC, 91)

Introduction

Thus far we have seen how the creation of a human subject with specific work and goal-intended actions is a limited countervailing power to sovereignty because it is inherent to the structure it tries to abolish. In this chapter emerges another attempt to develop a response to bare life and sovereign power: sacred life, that is, the claim that all life is sacred. Agamben shows that this response to the subordination of law is also insufficient and creates further problems.

The creation of bare life coheres closely with the creation of sacred life. Agamben used the concept of bare life to describe the politicization of physical life. Through the concept of 'sacred life' or the *homo sacer*, he elaborates on how life has become 'sacred' in politics, which resulted not in the protection of life, but in its juridical abandonment by removing it from the political order while at the same time keeping it at the centre of politics. This can be related to the original meaning of the word *sacer*. Whereas former chapters dealt with making the distinction between *zoē* and *bios* inoperative, this chapter will focus on the distinction between the sacred and profane and will begin by explaining the pitfalls of proclaiming life sacred.

Kafka's work contains various examples of strategies against the sacralization of life by making the distinction between sacred and profane inoperative. A good example is the condemned man in Kafka's 'In the Penal Colony', who lives in a kind of limbo: released without knowing he was condemned, this strategy will be described in 'Kafka's Limbo'. But the most fascinating strategy can be found in *The Castle* and in the profession of the main character K., the land surveyor. According to Agamben, this profession was an important one for the old Romans. A closer study of K.'s role in *The Castle* also provides further insight into the new Kabbalah that Kafka prepared and the end he saw for the higher powers and the functionaries of these powers.

The sacrality of life

Homo Sacer was Agamben's philosophical breakthrough. The protagonist of this book is, according to Agamben, 'bare life, that is, the life of *homo sacer* (sacred man), who *may be killed and yet not sacrificed* and whose essential function in modern politics we intend to assert' (HS, 8). In this passage, Agamben connects bare life with the *homo sacer*. Whereas bare life is the result of the inclusive-exclusive tension between simply being alive and the good life, *homo sacer* is the result of the inclusive-exclusive tension between the profane and the sacral world. If Agamben critically examines our use of the term 'life' through his concept 'bare life', he does this also for the terms 'sacral' and 'holy' through the concept *homo sacer*. Here also a certain resistance to metaphysics and transcendence can be detected.

In the previous chapter, we discussed Agamben's concept of 'bare life'. *Zoē* entered the *polis* in ancient Greece in the form of an inclusive exclusion, a state of exception. This led to a politicization of life and thus it was no longer simply *zoē*. *Zoē* entered the *polis* as bare life, in the margins of politics. The relation is that of a ban: politics continues to be involved in something that it has actually placed outside of its domain. The end of politics is, namely, the good life and not simply being alive. Aristotle describes *zoē*, simply being alive, as something to which people attach a certain value and that is the sense in which it is included in the *polis*, even if the good life is *bios*. From the perspective of the *polis*, however, *zoē* does not have much that is distinctively human about it and is thus of little value. Bare life emerges when *zoē* is politicized, when it becomes in the centre of politics. Since this bare life does not have many human characteristics, it can be killed easily. Bare life is created by politics, which hands it over to violence by the same gesture.

The Greek idea that 'simply being alive' is not worth very much and that it is abandoned to violence, quickly meets with resistance, especially in Jewish and Christian thinking. Benjamin describes this idea as the dogma of the sacrality of life: 'We, however, profess that higher even than the happiness and justice of existence stands existence itself.'[1] This differs from the Greek model, according to Agamben, because now *zoē*, natural life, is accorded the highest moral value and not *bios*. The reappraisal of *zoē* involves an attempt to remove it from its position in the periphery of the *polis*, by making *zoē* a form of life – *bios* – in itself: belonging to the human kind (natural life) should already be a 'form of life' (and thus important, fortunate, moral) in itself. Declaring *zoē* to be sacral, i.e. making *zoē* the highest good, results in the disappearance of the traditional distinction between life and good

[1] Benjamin, *Selected Writings 1*, 251.

life (*zoē* and *bios*). This does not separate *zoē* from the *polis*; rather, it degenerates into a complex hybrid with *bios*. And in Agamben's philosophy, complex, opaque hybrids always have complex, opaque and, in this case, violent consequences. 'When life and politics – originally divided and linked together by means of the no-man's-land of the state of exception that is inhabited by bare life – begin to become one, all life becomes sacred and all politics becomes the exception' (HS, 148).

The idea of sacrality is connected for the first time to human life in the Roman figure of the *homo sacer*. The Roman definition of *homo sacer* reads: 'The sacred man is the one whom the people have judged on account of a crime. It is not permitted to sacrifice this man, yet he who kills him will not be condemned for homicide' (HS, 71). Why this doctrine of the 'sacrality of life' does not protect the human being but only hands it over to violence can be explained, according to Agamben, by looking closer to the meaning of the work sacral.

Firstly, it is important to make a distinction between holy and sacral. The words *sanctus* (often translated as 'holy') and sacral both come from the root *sak*. *Sanctus* refers to a state of becoming whole and inviolable and is further removed from the root *sak* than sacral is. *Sacer* does not refer to an inviolable state of the individual (as does the word *sanctus*) but to its relation: not only to the *ius divinum*, but also to the *ius humanum*; not only to his god, but also and primarily to his fellow human beings. The root *sak* pointed originally to a place set apart and intended for a divinity, the sacral within the profane, a place of exception, a double exception, like an excrescence of the profane into the religious and of the religious into the profane. Understood in terms of its root *sak*, the word 'sacral' does not refer so much to a religious dimension as to setting the boundaries of the human community.

Returning to the definition of *homo sacer*, we can conclude the following: the double sense of the term *sacer* is that the person who is given this predicate is in principle excluded from the community, from the sphere of the profane (*ius humanum*) without falling under the *ius divinum*. 'Whoever kills him will not be condemned for murder' indicates that the *homo sacer* stands outside normal penal law, outside the *ius humanum*, which does view the killing of a free man as murder. 'It is not permitted to sacrifice him' indicates that the *homo sacer* is also not transferred to the sphere of the *ius divinum*. The inconsistency of the term *homo sacer* is solved on the basis of a non-religious interpretation of the word 'sacral', which refers to a place of exception in the social dimension, in which someone can, via the structure of the ban, be both included in and excluded from political life. That happens via and as a result of his unpunishable killing and the prohibition against sacrificing him. Agamben deduces the original meaning of the word *sacer* as 'doomed to die'. The attempt to declare life inviolable leads even more to its being handed over to an unpunishable killing. According to Agamben, in contemporary politics – seeing that we live in a permanent state of exception – we are all potential *homini sacri*: we can be killed at any moment without our killing being subject to punishment. So proclaiming life as sacred did not free it from sovereign power, but transformed it permanently into a state of exception.

Kafka's description of limbo situations, the steps the land surveyor takes and the redemption Kafka offers to God, the Count and the judges show us strategies we can use in response to the sacralization of life, to the creation of the *homo sacer*.

Kafka's limbo

If we re-evaluated Agamben's messianism in the light of the above explanation of *sanctus* and *sacer*, we see that Agamben's messianism is not so much a form of redemption as it is a redemption from salvation.[2] Redemption is not a matter of the profane becoming sacral or finding what was lost. Rather, redemption is the definitive profanation of the profane (CC, 101). In *Profanations*, Agamben places, over against the *homo sacer*, different creatures that escape sacrality and bare life, that are profanated. Examples of these creatures are children who have died before baptism and therefore exist in limbo. 'Irremediably lost, they persist without pain in divine abandon. God has not forgotten them, but rather they have always already forgotten God; and in the face of their forgetfulness, God's forgetting is impotent' (CC, 4-5). It is in that sense that they remove themselves from the inclusive exclusion and remain in a threshold of suspension in potentiality.

But Agamben finds another example of profanation in Kafka's story about the penal colony. Here an explorer discovers a penal colony in which a condemned man does not know he is condemned but will experience this verdict via a cruel instrument of torture and execution. The officer of the penal colony, however, decides to release the condemned man (who does not know he has been condemned and stares full of curiosity at the instrument of torture) and to take his place. This leads to the destruction of the machine (we will return to this in Chapter 8). Agamben cites this story as an example of a limbo, of redemption from salvation of profanated lives.

[2] DelaDurantaye, *Agamben*, 199.

> Like the freed convict in Kafka's penal colony, who has survived the destruction of the machine that was to have executed him, these beings have left the world of guilt and justice behind them: The light that rains down on them is that irreparable light of the dawn following the *novissima dies* of judgement. But the life that begins on earth after the last day is simply human life. (CC, 5-6)

Agamben sees a parallel here with the non-baptized children in limbo – the man is not simply saved, but is redeemed from salvation; he can be his 'simply human life', not sacred life, not bare life. So as Agamben transformed the virtual state of exception into the real state of exception, imperfect nihilism to perfect nihilism, in the same gesture he reverses the threshold that the *homo sacer* creates into a limbo of simply human life. Agamben cites yet another example from Kafka's works of how the threshold in which the *homo sacer* finds himself – excluded from society but not transferred to the divine order – can be reversed, namely in Kafka's *The Castle*.

The steps of the land surveyor

Kafka's story *The Castle* opens as follows:

> It was late evening when K. arrived. The village lay under deep snow. There was no sign of the Castle hill, fog and darkness surrounded it, not even the faintest gleam of light suggested the large Castle. K. stood a long time on the wooden bridge that leads from the main road to the village, gazing upward into the seeming emptiness.

He finds refuge for the night in an inn. Since there are no more rooms available, he gets a straw mattress in the taproom. K. falls asleep, but only to be awakened shortly after that by the son of the Castle steward, who says to him:

> This village is Castle property, anybody residing or spending the night here is effectively residing or spending the night at the Castle. Nobody may do so without permission from the Count. But you have no such permission or at least you haven't shown it yet.

K. introduces himself as the land surveyor sent for by the Count. The young man then decides to call the castle. Initially, it is denied that the Count ordered a land surveyor, but shortly after the young man ends the phone conversation, the phone rings again and the ordering of the land surveyor is confirmed. K. listens intently. So the Castle had appointed him land surveyor.

> On one hand, this was unfavourable, for it showed that the Castle had all necessary information about him, had assessed the opposing forces and was taking up the struggle with a smile. On the other hand, it was favourable, for it proved to his mind that they underestimated him and that he would enjoy greater freedom than he could have hoped for at the beginning. And if they thought they could keep him terrified all the time simply by acknowledging his surveyorship – though this was certainly a superior move on their part – then they were mistaken, for he felt only a slight shudder, that was all.[3]

In the rest of the story, K. attempts in vain to get into the castle to receive further instructions and in the meantime struggles with the mistrust of the villagers. The story ends abruptly – the German edition even ends in the middle of a sentence. Kafka died before he could finish *The Castle*, but he told Brod the end he had in mind: K. dies of frustration and exhaustion without ever meeting the Count.

Just like other stories by Kafka, *The Castle* at first glance primarily seems to contain a depressing description of the bureaucracy to which human beings are subjected. The castle, 'which burdens the village with the obscurity of its decrees and the multiplicity of its offices', has the village in its power (MWC, 108). Just as Benjamin already remarked, life as it is lived in the village at the foot of the mountain can no longer be distinguished from the law (SE, 63). But, like many other stories by Kafka, *The Castle* also contains a strategy and the main character K. is not as powerless as he seems. His strategy, according to Agamben, lies primarily in his profession: land surveyor.

K. the land surveyor

K. introduces himself at the inn as a land surveyor and sees that this causes confusion for the representatives of the Castle. Why is that? The profession of land surveyor was of special importance in old Rome, according to Agamben. Land surveyors were charged with establishing boundaries. In both civil and public law, the practise of the law consisted in the possibility of marking the boundaries of territories, demarcating and allocating land and, finally, resolving boundary conflicts. That is why the land surveyor was also called the creator of the law. For the Romans, the heavenly character of establishing boundaries was beyond question: boundaries are established in accordance with how the world is, by following the course of the sun and the axes of the poles (K, 22).

[3] Kafka, *The Castle*, 1-5.

K.'s profession, the profession that he announces provocatively to the functionaries of the castle and that he takes upon himself as a kind of challenge, is the 'establishment of the boundaries'. Agamben contends that Kafka's novella *The Castle* is not about 'settling down in a village and being accepted by the castle' (as Kafka's friend Max Brod claims) but about establishing (or transgressing) boundaries. If the castle, according to Brod, serves as the 'divine governance' of the world, then the surveyor – who is introduced without instruments although he does have a knobby walking stick within reach – is involved in a struggle between the castle and its functionaries on the limits of this governance, in a final and very special establishment of the boundaries (K, 23–4).

The meaning of the boundary or threshold in Agamben

Agamben is not thinking about territorial boundaries when he uses the term 'boundary'. Murray points out that these boundaries are not physical but categorical.[4] The role of politics is to decide continuously about boundaries – boundaries between life and death, public and private, citizens and non-citizens. But precisely because these boundaries have entered the political domain, they are unclear and contested and they present themselves to us as questions, a thing that the law does and can neither recognize nor accept. Let us look, for example, at the boundaries between life and death. Bearers of political rights are primarily living people. But when is someone 'living'? Since conception? After three months after conception? After birth? When is someone dead? When he is brain-dead? When all vital functions have ceased? Or we could look at the boundaries between private and public life. How far is politics allowed to go in interfering in the private lives of people? Is the decision about the life of a person in a coma or a seriously challenged child a private or a political decision? The boundaries between citizens and non-citizens raise questions as well. Who is eligible to be protected by national law? Everyone with a passport provided under such a law? Can passports be withdrawn once given out, in particular from naturalized citizens (as compared to right of birth)? Historically, there are many instances in which these questions have been answered by the violence of the law, with as the obvious example the way in which Nazi Germany systematically took away the civil rights of Jews until eventually their status as human beings was denied.

Who must be protected as a citizen and who is an enemy of the state? Who is responsible when citizens are marked 'unjustly' as enemies of the

4 Murray, *Agamben*, 105.

state (a risk of which we are all potentially in danger), especially in crisis situations after terrorist attacks or after the anarchy that follows natural violence? (For example, after Hurricane Katrina, some people were unjustly marked as enemies of the state because of alleged plundering and lawlessness and were treated as such).[5]

The problem of establishing these boundaries is that they cannot be drawn sharply. In an attempt to draw these boundaries, a large grey area appears in which the distinction between the two poles disappears, resulting in a strong dehumanization of the lives in the border zone. Politics mostly does not know how to handle these grey areas and this shortcoming results in establishing camps like asylum seeker centres, refugee camps, Guantánamo Bay, Abu Ghraib and concentration camps. The attempt to establish the boundaries nonetheless often leads to a situation of exclusive inclusion, a border situation.

Since politics decides who is human and who is not, who is a citizen and who is an enemy of the state, any determining of the boundaries creates a state of exception and makes the lines between law and lawlessness fade away. In that light, the surveyor has an important task in disputing the boundaries set by the state.

The boundary or threshold in Kafka's work

That making boundaries inoperative may be an important theme for Kafka is, according to Agamben, shown by a journal entry that Kafka wrote while he worked on *The Castle*. On 16 January 1922, Kafka wrote about a breakdown he had experienced the week before. He describes the confusion that he consequently experienced as a 'pursuit' (*Jagen*), an image that opens up the way for a reflection on the boundary between the human being and what is above or outside of him:

> 'Pursuit', indeed, is only an image. I can also say 'assault on the last earthly frontier', an assault, moreover, launched from below, from mankind and since this too is an image, I can replace it by the image of an assault from above, aimed at me from above. All such writing is an assault on the frontiers; if Zionism had not intervened, it might easily have developed into a new secret doctrine, a Kabbalah. There are intimations of this.[6]

That this is a meaningful passage in Kafka's work has been underscored many times, but without bringing it into connection with the profession of

[5] See, for example, the controversial novel *Zeitoun* by Dave Eggers.
[6] Kafka, *Diaries*, 150–1, cited in K, 24, translation adapted by Agamben.

the protagonist of the novel. The assault on the last earthly frontiers can be developed into a new secret teaching: a way out (K, 25).

If we connect this journal entry with the land surveyor K. ('he who is oriented to the poles of the heavens'), this journal entry gains extra meaning. The careful choice of profession and his appropriation of this task for which no one has appointed him – because, as the village chairman tells him, land surveyors are not needed in the village – are at the same time a summons to war and a strategy. The concern here is not with the boundaries between the gardens and the houses of the village that, in the words of the chairman, have already been correctly marked and registered, a task he oversaw. Rather, more fundamental power boundaries between the village and the castle are disturbed by the surveyor's coming, given that life in the village is in reality completely determined by the boundaries that divide it from the castle – and keep it connected to it at the same time. The 'assault on the last frontier' is an attack on the boundaries that divide the castle (the high) from the village (the low) (K, 25).

Kafka's greatest strategic intuition, the new Kabbalah that he is preparing, is that the struggle is not against God or the highest sovereign power (Count West-West does not actually play any role in the novel) but against the messengers and the functionaries who apparently represent him. It is not a question of a conflict with the divine, but of a conflict with the productions of the human being concerning the divine: the system of laws, written and unwritten, that regulate the relation between the high and the low, the divine and the human, the pure and the impure. It is these productions of people, the divisions and the boundaries that they set up between people themselves and between people and the divine, that the surveyor questions, that he wants to cancel – or, better, make inoperative or neutralize. For no one seems to know where this boundary is found in material terms; perhaps it does not exist in reality, but it runs like an invisible door through every living being (K, 26).

Kafka's new Kabbalah: Redemption for God, the count and the judges

In one of his recent books, *The Kingdom and the Glory*, Agamben takes an unexpected turn. Whereas in *Homo Sacer* the sovereign power was the antagonist of bare life, Agamben suddenly shifts his attention in *The Kingdom and the Glory* from the sovereign power to those who execute that power. Agamben moves from the sovereign power to the practise of governing (*gouvermentalité*). The actual problem is, according to Agamben, not sovereignty but government, not the king but the minister, not the law but the power of the police, i.e. the state machine that they constitute and maintain.

Analogous to the idea of 'being in force without significance' is the sovereign or the king as someone who rules but does not govern. Agamben cites, for example, the Fisher King of the Grail legend. This king has a war wound in his thigh that prevents him from standing up or getting on a horse – signs of worldly power. If he wants to be amused, then he is put into a boat and goes fishing while his falconers, archers and hunters fight one another over their territory in the woods. Agamben sees a parallel in this story with a version of Kafka's story of the young hunter Gracchus, in which the hunter-king Gracchus becomes separated from his dogs and hunters while hunting in the woods. He comes to a bank and finds a boat, in which is a shining sword. When he attempts to draw the sword from its sheath, he wounds himself in his thighs. These images of a mutilated king contains a kind of anticipation of the modern sovereign who 'rules but does not govern' (KG, 68–9).

The sovereign as being in force without significance, as a ruler who does not govern, finds an echo in the following fragment by Kafka:

> They were given the choice of becoming kings or the kings' messengers. As is the way with children, they all wanted to be messengers. That is why there are only messengers, racing through the world and, since there are no kings, calling out to each other the messages that have now become meaningless. They would gladly put an end to their miserable life, but they do not dare to do so because of their oath of loyalty.[7]

Another example in Kafka's stories is the messenger who has to deliver the final message from the emperor who has just died. The messenger, however, will never reach his destination.[8] But if the sovereign rules but does not govern, who then governs? Agamben finds a hint in the theological hypothesis that not God but the angels govern the earth. As those who execute God's will (who is in force but has no significance), the angels are grouped into a kind of royal court similar to Kafka's castle and where the functionaries are categorized in such a way as to indicate their distance from the sovereign. In Agamben's view, this hierarchy shows that the difference between the angels and the bureaucrats disappears, as becomes clear in

[7] Kafka, *Octavo Notebooks*, 28.
[8] Kafka, *Selected Stories*, 120.

Kafka's stories: the bureaucrats receive higher powers and the higher powers interfere more and more with earthly matters (KG, 157).

> It is the similarity between angels and bureaucrats that the greatest theologian of the twentieth century, Franz Kafka, understood and showed with a somnambulistic precision, when he had his officials, messengers and assistants act like angels in disguise. (VBH, 13–14)

It is surprising, Agamben contends, that the two writers who in our century observed the incomparable horror that surrounded them with the greatest clarity – Kafka and Walser – present to us a world in which evil in its traditional form *par excellence*, the demonic, has disappeared (CC, 30). Kafka's notion of evil lies, according to Agamben, close to that of Spinoza, who wrote that the demon is the one who 'is the most vulnerable of all creatures and the furthest removed from God and as such – that is, insofar as the demon is essentially impotent – cannot only not do any evil but, in contrast to that, is the one who has most need of our help and our prayers' (CC, 30). This leads Agamben to the following definition of a demon: 'The demon constitutes in every being the possibility of not being that, in silence, needs our help.' Evil in Kafka's work is more a matter of our response to our own impotence, or our inability for impotentiality. One of the problems is that we respond to our impotentiality by attempting to exercise power over being (CC, 31). By performing the work of the sovereign, establishing boundaries, we are all potential sovereigns; we are all tempted to take the role of the doorkeeper.

From the above, it appears that the law, the power, is in a crisis: it is in force but no longer has any significance. It attempts to create a subject that it can subordinate to itself, whereas the true identity of the subject continually eludes the law's divisions. Agamben's rejection of metaphysical transcendence sets the idea of power and oppression in a new light. Following Foucault, it is not so much a matter of a static division but of a relation. Although the previous chapters were written primarily from the point of view of a repressed subject who attempts to wrest himself free from subjectification, what is at issue here is actually the relation to both ways: the subject and the sovereign power. The change in the relation influences both parties: not only is the subject in a crisis, but power is also. In Kafka's work this is reflected by the fact that the sovereign power or the antagonists stay out of sight; no clearly identifiable counterweight can be found, no identifiable actor. It remains unclear as to who counteracted, who slandered, who accused.

Agamben holds that it is not Joseph K. in *The Trial* or K. in *The Castle* who must be helped or saved, but the sovereign power itself, God and those who execute that power:

> [T]he only happy ending we can imagine for his novels is the redemption of Klamm, of the Count, of the anonymous, theological crowd of judges, lawyers and guardians indiscriminately packed together in dusty corridors or stooped beneath oppressive ceiling. (IP, 85)

Kafka's new Kabbalah is an assault on the boundary between the subject and power. In this assault on the boundary, not only is the subject given back its being-thus, but the power and the executors of that power are also dissolved. At the moment that it has lost power over its subject, the boundaries also disappear. 'What changes are not the things but their limits' (CC, 91).

We will now end this discussion here, i.e. the struggle between power and the attribution of an identity and transcendence to the subject, so that we can look at two other aspects of metaphysical politics: language and time. This will add sharper lines to the way out for the subject.

7

Strategies in Response to Language

Man exists in language like a fly trapped in a bottle: that which it cannot see is precisely that through which it sees the world.

(Wittgenstein)[1]

Introduction

Although it does not seem a very obvious connection at first, Agamben's political analysis is closely connected with his philosophy of language and he sees the same problems in language that he describes in politics. Language is based on the same inclusive exclusion structure as the state of exception and reflects the same metaphysical assumptions that can be found in politics. Our understanding of language traps us in this metaphysical conception of the world. But Agamben also sees language as an important possibility. He also makes a number of essential references to Kafka in his philosophy of language, especially with respect to finding a way out of the metaphysical structures of language. The strategies for dealing with language focus on two aspects of language: its presuppositional structure and its ability to define identity which can result in inclusive exclusion.

Agamben describes different strategies in relation to the presuppositional structure of language. Kafka's story of the return of the person in suspended animation shows how language can make its relation to transcendence – to the idea that there is 'something outside language' to which language refers – inoperative. Kafka's description of the impatience of those who have been banished from paradise also shows the way in which the impossible desire for transcendence can not only be a matter of fate, but also of salvation. This impatience is deeply rooted in literature, as a search for a language to grasp the world. Agamben shows via a journal entry by Kafka on magic how the subject can be liberated from language and his parable on parables shows how one can become language, thus making the distinction between language and subject inoperative.

[1] Wittgenstein, cited in DelaDurantaye, *Agamben*, 93.

A strategy that aims directly at the political function of language, language as administering justice and exclusion, can be found in Kafka's story 'In the Penal Colony'. This story reveals an important messianic component of language and an inversion of the meaning of language.

Language as presupposition and exclusion

The main motive behind Agamben's philosophy is language rather than politics: 'In both my written and unwritten books, I have stubbornly pursued only one train of thought: what is the meaning of "there is language"; what is the meaning of "I speak"?' (IH, 5). With these words Agamben characterizes his own work and, although this seems perhaps to be a surprising expression for most readers of *Homo Sacer*, his philosophy of language is thoroughly interwoven into his work and can indeed be seen as one of his core themes.

Language and presupposition

One important characteristic of language, according to Agamben, is that it is based on the presupposition of a subject to which it refers. Aristotle argued that language, 'saying something about something', necessarily brings about a distinction between a first 'something' (a subject) and a second 'something' (a predicate). And this is meaningful only if the first 'something' is presupposed. This subject, the immediate, the non-linguistic, is a presupposition of language. At the same time, language seems to precede the subject it presupposes; the world can only be known through language. That there is language that gives meaning and facilitates the transmission of this meaning is a presupposition that precedes every communication because communication always begins with language.[2]

Agamben compares our relationship with language with Wittgenstein's image of a fly in a bottle: 'Man exists in language like a fly trapped in a bottle: that which it cannot see is precisely that through which it sees the world.'[3] According to Agamben, contemporary thought has recognized that we are imprisoned within the limits of the presuppositional structure of language, within this glass. But contemporary thought has not seen that it is possible to leave the glass (PO, 46).

> Our age does indeed stand in front of language just as the man from the country in the parable stands in front of the door of the Law. What

[2] Daniel Heller-Roazen, 'To Read What Was Never Written'. In *Potentialities. Collected Essays in Philosophy*, edited by Daniel Heller-Roazen. (Stanford, CA: Stanford University Press, 1999), 2.

[3] Idem.

> threatens thinking here is the possibility that thinking might find itself condemned to infinite negotiations with the doorkeeper or, even worse, that it might end by itself assuming the role of the doorkeeper who, without really blocking the entry, shelters the Nothing onto which the door opens. (HS, 54)

Agamben sees a way out of language described in many of Kafka's stories, but before we proceed to that, let us first look at the relationship between language and politics. In addition to the meaning of 'there is language', Agamben is also searching for the meaning of 'I speak', the relationship between language and subject and the attempt of language to name a subject, to define its identity.

Language and exclusion

In *Language and Death*, Agamben questions the essential relation that metaphysics proposes between the human being and language. Aristotle was one of the first to highlight language as the most important feature of human being and since the goal of politics was to make human life flourish, language incorporates humans in the *polis*:

> Among living beings, only man has language. The voice is the sign of pain and pleasure and this is why it belongs to other living beings (since their nature has developed to the point of having the sensations of pain and pleasure and of signifying the two). But language is for manifesting the fitting and the unfitting and the just and the unjust. To have the sensation of the good and the bad and of the just and the unjust is what is proper to men as opposed to other living beings and the community of these things makes dwelling and the city.[4]

Aristotle makes a distinction here between *phonè* and *logos*, between voice (natural element) and language (human element), that is very similar to the distinction between *zoē* and *bios*. In the same way as the distinction between *zoē* and *bios* is responsible for the creation of bare life, the distinction between *phonè* and *logos* also indicates an inclusive exclusion, this time through language. Agamben sees a close connection here between language and bare life:

> The question 'In what way does the living being have language?' corresponds exactly to the question 'In what way does bare life dwell in the *polis*?' … There is politics because man is the living being who, in

[4] Aristotle, *Ethica*, 1253a, cited in HS, 7–8.

> language, separates and opposes himself to his own bare life and, at the same time, maintains himself in relation to that bare life in an inclusive exclusion. (HS, 7-8)

This inclusive-exclusion structure, this ban relationship, is similar for law and language. Although language is inadequate to capture the subject, one cannot step out of it in order to do right to the things that cannot be said in language.[5]

Here the presuppositional structure of language comes back again. Since language presupposes the subject, while at the same time it cannot fully grasp it and the human subject is the goal of law, language and law are tightly connected in an incomplete presentation of the human being. In that way, language constitutes sovereign power and functions in the same way.[6]

> Language is the sovereign who, in a permanent state of exception, declares that there is nothing outside language and that language is always beyond itself. The particular structure of law has its foundation in this presuppositional structure of human language. It expresses the bond of inclusive exclusion to which a thing is subject because of the fact of being in language, of being named. To speak [*dire*]is, in this sense, always to speak the law, *ius dicere*. (HS, 21)

In the sense that language is connected to biopolitics and bare life, it is also connected to death. Agamben quotes Heidegger: 'Mortals are they who can experience death as death. Animals cannot do so. But animals cannot speak either. The essential relation between death and language flashes up before us, but remains still unthought.'[7]

Thus, one of the main problems of language is the definition of the human being as *zoon logon echon*, i.e. the living being that has language.[8] Both language and politics abandon the human being to death with their attempt to define the human being.[9] This close connection between language and politics, between speaking and 'speak the law', or the articulation of a verdict,[10] comes to light in Kafka's story 'In the Penal Colony'. This story also

[5] Liska, 'The Messiah before the Law', 165.

[6] The most recent part of the *Homo Sacer* cycle, which is intended to provide an overview of sovereign power, has to do with language. In *The Sacrament of Language*, Agamben brings to light a 'sacral' connection between human beings and language, between language and the *homo sacer* (Colby Dickinson, *Agamben and Theology*, New York: Continuum, 2011, 37).

[7] Heidegger, cited in LD, xi.

[8] Mills, *The Philosophy of Agamben*, 45.

[9] Ibid., 58.

[10] See HS, 21: 'To speak [*dire*] is, in this sense, always to speak the law," *ius dicere*.' This connection is also partially discussed in Chapter 1, in which the relation between law and pronouncing a verdict is exposed.

contains a strategy to give language a new meaning past its political function as death machine.

Kafka's story on the return of the person in suspended animation, his ideas on impatience, magic names and the justness of the officer in the penal colony, can be read as strategies against the presuppositional structure of language and the political function of language.

The return of the person in suspended animation

Agamben sees a close relationship between Kafka's story of the return of the person in suspended animation and the presuppositional structure of language. The story reveals an important strategy against this presuppositional structure; this is how it goes:

> Anyone who has once been in a state of suspended animation can tell terrible stories about it, but he cannot say what it is like after death, he has actually been no nearer to death than anyone else, fundamentally he has only 'lived' through an extraordinary experience and not-extraordinary, everyday life has become more valuable to him as a result.[11]

If we experience something special, Kafka claims, we do not want to dwell in the experience so much as return as quickly as possible. According to Kafka, it is this possibility of return that is decisive. The person in suspended animation has in reality never been dead, or else he would not have been able to return.

> [F]rom those who have returned from a state of suspended animation … one can learn a great deal, but the decisive thing cannot be discovered from them, for they themselves have not discovered [it]. If they had discovered it, they would not have come back at all.[12]

Our desire for extraordinary experiences is only to experience them if we are assured that we will be able to return, if we have a safeguard. The reason for this, according to Kafka, does not have to do with the fear of death directly but with the possibility of return.

In one of his first works on Kafka – indeed, one of his first publications – Agamben takes up this story by Kafka more closely. Firstly, he sees in this story an argument for radical immanence instead of transcendence: 'We can, in fact, only have knowledge about that from which we can return, but the

[11] Kafka, *Octavo Notebooks*, 392.

[12] Ibid., 392.

things we can return from are not really beyond the world and everyday life' (QGK, 37). Agamben also argues, following Kafka, that it is not so much the extraordinary experience itself that is decisive as the moment of return.

Agamben describes suspended animation as 'a return from where we never have been' and argues that language has the same structure. Although language has no 'outside itself', it does claim it, just as the person in suspended animation claims to have really been dead. And this is precisely what Agamben is arguing against in his philosophy of language. For him, there is nothing 'outside' language.[13]

> The word, of course, has never been outside of the word, in the non-linguistic and it is useless to desire this for it; if it had been, then we would not have been able to talk about it, it would no longer be word. The same non-linguistic, the same inexpressible, is, indeed, nothing more than an invention of the word. (QGK, 37–8)

But Kafka's story about suspended animation and especially the return, is not only a paradigm to show that language is an unceasing return before having been anywhere, before having been really outside language. Agamben also sees here an important insight through which we can liberate ourselves from the presuppositional structure of language:

> But, at the point where we understand the word as word, we cease to imagine words beyond the word, we cease to pretend that we have been truly death. Back from where we never were, we are finally here, where we can no longer return. The non-linguistic, unspoken in the word, is now fully sayable. (QGK, 38)

It does not so much concern the extraordinary as it does the return to the ordinary with the sense that there is no extraordinary. Twenty-five years after his interpretation of Kafka's suspended animation in 'Quattro Glosse a Kafka', Agamben returned to the relation between language, death and return in *Language and Death* (1991). Agamben describes philosophy as the return of the word to itself. 'The word must return to itself and, absolving itself of this scission, it must be at the end there where, without knowing it, it was already in the beginning' (LD, 93). Language returns to what it never was and what it never left (LD, 97). Agamben quotes a poem by Caproni, which echoes Benjamin's parable of the coming of the Messiah where everything will stay the same, just a little bit different. In the same way, the return is also a special kind of movement:

[13] Daniel McLoughlin, 'The Politics of Caesura: Giorgio Agamben on Language and the Law'. *Law and Critique* 20, no. 2 (2009), 174.

> I returned there
> Where I have never been
> Nothing has changed from how it was not.
> On the table (on the checkered
> Tablecloth) half-full
> I found the glass
> Which was never filled. All
> Has remained just as
> I never left it. (cited in LD, 98)

In 'The Thing Itself' Agamben describes the idea of the return of language as circular: the place of arrival is the point of departure (TI, 22). But what has changed is that the subject of language (the thing itself) is no longer simply an obscure entity, an object that is presupposed by language, it now shows its being-thus, its knowability (TI, 22–3).

> The thing itself has, therefore, its eminent place in language, even if language is undoubtedly not perfectly suited to it, because, as Plato puts it, of its weakness. It could be said, with an apparent paradox, that even while transcending language in some way, the thing itself is possible only in language and by virtue of language – the *thing of language*, as it were. (TI, 21)

The thing itself is not a different thing, but the same thing. It is just no longer presupposed or placed under language, as an obscure presupposition. Rather, it is replaced in the medium of its own knowability (TI, 23). There is a strong affinity between Agamben's idea of return and the inversion that Camus and Benjamin show exists in Kafka's work. It is not an inversion into something completely different but an inversion that changes both everything and nothing. Kafka's idea of the return shows the possibility of making the presuppositional structure of language inoperative and opens the way to a correct use of language beyond language, the word beyond the word.

So the first strategy with regard to language as presupposition resembles, in some sense, the inversion of the law's being in force without significance. The circular movement of the person in suspended animation transforms language in a being-thus, a radical immanence of language, an indistinguishability between language and the thing itself. The second strategy looks at the implications of immanent language for literature.

The impatience of literature

The split between sign and what is signified, between language and what language presupposes, has divided language into two different discourses, practised, for example, by philosophy and poetry. But both are mutilated, according to Agamben, as a result of this split: philosophy aims at the truth but has no instrument to convey it and poetry focuses on the instrument and not so much on truth. Both disciplines fall short: 'Poetry possesses its object without knowing it while philosophy knows its object without possessing it' (S, xvii). Agamben wonders if a new use of language can be found and places his hopes on a number of writers who are difficult to place in either the category of philology or that of the poetic use of language, writers like Kafka, Benjamin and Hölderlin, who, in Agamben's view, have made the caesurae in language the place where they work. One of the characteristics of Kafka's writings is that he made the margin between truth and its transmission his central experience (IH, 164). DeNicola describes how Kafka's use of language undermines the structuralistic relationship between the sign and what is signified and exposes the inherent metaphysics behind it.[14] Because of this, his work does not come to a conclusive and definitive judgement, but is a 'radical undecidability and perpetual becoming'. Kafka's work 'does not seek at closure, but is comfortable meandering in the space of infinite suspension'.[15]

According to Agamben, literature is a search for this form of language that no longer has any transcendent meaning. Agamben sees literature as sick of impatience and this sickness is both its fate as well as its way out. It is its fate because in this attempt it cannot step outside its own contradiction, there is no meaning of language; the quest for language leads only to silence and the quest for significance only to non-significance.

> Thus, literature becomes a parabola of a significance, trying to give itself a form, create a sign and get lost because of this creation and believes it has found itself while being lost; but once tired of its own game, then devours this sign in an atrocious impatience regarding itself and is thus again led to its point of departure. (PB, 48)

In its patience, literature seems to have forgotten that its fate is precisely the unattainability of its own paradise. At the same time, this is also what its impatience helps literature remember and, in that sense, impatience is a

[14] Paul DeNicola, 'Literature as Pure Mediality: Kafka and the Scene of Writing'. *The European Graduate School* (2007), 99.

[15] Ibid., 118; 46.

way out: literature owes its significance precisely to its lack of significance. In order to make a euporia from this aporia, literature has to follow this blind alley to its end and not only in an attempt to find a paradise.

For Agamben, this is also the meaning of Kafka's aphorism in 'Reflections on Sin, Pain, Hope and the True Way':

> There are two main human sins from which all the others derive: impatience and indolence. It was because of impatience that they were expelled from Paradise; it is because of indolence that they do not return. Yet perhaps there is only one major sin: impatience. Because of impatience they were expelled, because of impatience they do not return.[16]

In this aphorism, impatience is, on the one hand, what made us lose transcendence and paradise and, on the other hand, because we cannot return out of our impatience, the transcendence becomes a radical immanence.

Agamben describes another example from Kafka's work in which language is disconnected from transcendent meaning, namely Kafka's description of Yiddish as a 'minor language', a jargon. Agamben sees this as a language beyond grammatical language and claims that 'there is nothing more genuinely Jewish than to inhabit a language of exile and to labor it from within, up to the point of confounding its very identity and turning it into more than just a grammar' (TR, 4–5). What does this language looks like? Agamben recalls an anecdote by Jacob Taubes, a rabbi who worked with Scholem. Once, Taubes was talking to the Germanist Emil Staiger, who told him that he was reading the letters of the apostle Paul. But he added bitterly that he did not view them as having been written in Greek, but in Yiddish. Taubes replied: '[T]hat is why I can understand them'.

To summarize, the second strategy against the presuppositional structure of language walks through the blind alley of the nihilism of language in order to stay in a margin between truth and transmission, an impatience that turned a longing for transcendence into a dwelling in pure immanence. The next strategy looks at the relationship between being and language.

Kafka's becoming language and magical names

If we return to the previously described strategy of return to dismantle the presuppositional structure of language, what can this return do for the

[16] Franz Kafka, 'Reflections on Sin, Pain, Hope and the True Way'. In *The Great Wall of China. Stories and Reflections*. (New York: Schocken Books, 1970), 87.

subject that is subordinated in language and thus in law? Agamben outlines the same structure of return and language in his description of the parable as a genre. In the parable, the distinction between *signum* (sign) and *res significa* (that which is signified) tends to annul itself without completely disappearing (TR, 43). What is compared in the parable, as for example in the messianic parables in the gospel of Matthew, is not only the kingdom of God with the terms used in the parables (a field in which wheat and weeds are mixed), but the discourse about the kingdom and the kingdom itself. In that sense, the messianic parables in Matthew are parables about language, for what is meant is language itself. And this, according to Agamben, is also the meaning of Kafka's parable 'On Parables'. Kafka is looking for a way beyond language that is only possible by becoming language itself; beyond the distinction between sign and what is signified:

> If you'd follow the parables, you'd become parables yourselves and with that, free of the everyday struggle. (TR, 43)[17]

What Kafka indicates here, according to Agamben, is an indistinguishability between being and language. What does this process of becoming language look like? Agamben sees a hint of this in one of Kafka's journal entries. On 18 October 1921, Kafka wrote in his journal:

> Life calls again. It is entirely conceivable that life's splendor forever lies in wait about each one of us in all its fullness, but veiled from view, deep down, invisible, far off. It is there, though, not hostile, not reluctant, not deaf. If you summon it by the right word, by its right name, it will come. This is the essence of magic, which does not create but summons.[18]

According to Agamben, this refers to an old tradition followed by the Kabbalists in which magic is, in essence, a science of secret names. Everything has its apparent name and a hidden name and those who know this hidden name have power over life and death and the death of those to whom this name belongs. But, Agamben proposes, there is also another tradition that holds that this secret name is not so much the key by which the magician can gain power over a subject as it is a monogram by which things can be liberated from language. The secret name is the name the being received in Eden. If it is spoken aloud, all its apparent names fall away; the whole Babel of names disappears. 'To have a name is to be guilty. And justice, like magic, is nameless' (P, 22). The secret name is the gesture that restores the creature to the unexpressed. Thus, Agamben argues, magic is not the secret

[17] Kafka, *Selected Stories*, 162.
[18] Kafka, *Diaries*, 18 October 1921.

knowledge of names and their transcendent meaning, but a breaking free from the name. 'Happy and without a name, the creature knocks at the gates of the land of the magi, who speaks in gestures alone' (P, 22).

To summarize, the third strategy against the presuppositional structure of language is to follow the metaphysical assumptions regarding language to their extreme, until an indistinguishability occurs between the subject and language, a becoming language, a freeing of one's identity from the Babel of names. While this strategy was described from the perspective of the subject, the second strategy is described from power that is captured in the same metaphysical structure.

The justness of the officer in the penal colony

In the penal colony

In Kafka's story 'In the Penal Colony', Agamben sees a strategy against language as a form of political exclusion. In this story, an explorer discovers a penal colony in a deep, sandy, small valley. He is invited by the officer of the penal colony to attend the execution of a prisoner, an offer that he accepts out of politeness. The officer is eager to show the explorer how the machine that will be used to carry out the execution works. The machine stands beside a pit of earth that has been excavated. It consists of a bed, covered with a layer of cotton wool, on which the condemned man will be tied naked and on his stomach. The scriber is erected two metres above the bed and between the scriber and the bed is a steel band, the harrow. The harrow will carry out the execution. The command that the condemned man broke will be engraved on his body by the harrow. But it is essential that the condemned man does not know the sentence; the condemned man does not even know he is condemned.

The officer explains to the explorer that the principle that determines his sentence is: 'Guilt is always beyond all doubt'.[19] According to the officer, there was no purpose in interrogating someone and giving him the time to defend himself:

> If I had first summoned the man and interrogated him, it would only have led to confusion. He would have lied; if I had succeeded in refuting these lies, he would have substituted new lies for them and so forth.[20]

[19] Kafka, *Selected Stories,* 40.
[20] Ibid., 41.

It is also pointless to tell him the sentence, seeing that he is going to experience it on his own body. The needles of the harrow engrave the sentence in the back of the condemned man. The harrow goes deeper and deeper and for the first six hours the condemned man will suffer a great deal of pain. But after six hours, a turning point is reached: the sentence is then written in a writing that cannot be deciphered with the eyes, but only with wounds. After six hours, the condemned man succeeds in deciphering the writing. The moment of the sixth hour is especially significant for the spectators because a glow begins to spread over his whole face when the condemned man begins to understand the sentence.

> But how quiet the man becomes around the sixth hour! Understanding dawns even on the dumbest. It begins around the eyes. From there it spreads. A sight that could seduce one to lie down alongside him under the harrow. Nothing more actually happens, the man merely begins to decipher the script, he purses his lips as if he were listening hard.[21]

The condemned man deciphers the script for the next six hours, after which he dies because he is entirely skewered and then thrown into the pit.

In his interpretation of the story, Agamben argues that Kafka's story can be explained only if one understands that the torture apparatus that was invented by the officer of the colony is really language. The machine is, moreover, an instrument to condemn and to punish, just as language is primarily a matter of 'speaking the law' or the articulation of a verdict: naming of subjects in order to bring them into politics via an exclusion. 'Language is the punishment. All things must enter it and perish there according to the scale of their sin' (IP, 115).

If language has the function of 'speaking the law' and punishing, what is the punishment that is imposed? The punishment is to experience the presuppositional structure of language: that the subject is included in language only via its exclusion. Agamben argues:

> What the condemned man thus manages to grasp in the silence of his last hour is the meaning of language. … It is not a matter, of course, of grasping a logical sense, something one could read with one's eyes; but of a deeper meaning that can only be made out by one's wounds and that belongs to language only as punishment. (IP, 116)

'Men', Agamben states, 'live their lives as speaking beings without understanding the meaning at issue' (IP, 116). What the condemned man silently understands in his final hour is the significance of language, its

[21] Ibid., 44–5.

presuppositional structure, carried out to the extreme. He becomes aware of a deeper significance that reveals that language can function only as a lethal machine.[22]

The messianic inversion of language in the penal colony

The first half of Agamben's interpretation of Kafka's story 'In the Penal Colony' is not very hopeful. But Agamben's philosophy of language is closely related to his philosophy of potentiality and messianism.[23] While Agamben wrote in 1989 that the central theme in his work is language, he stated three years earlier in a lecture on potentiality that the central theme in his work was to understand what the signficance of the verb 'can' (*potere*) was. 'What do I mean when I say: "I can, I cannot"?' (PO, 177). Language contains a messianic potential, since a core element of messianic thinking is the introduction of the coming liberation from the law and the removal of the sign structure in language.[24] Agamben's search for language is also a search for the way out he sees in this language. Just as Agamben often reads in Kafka's stories a possibility of converting the state of exception into a real state of exception, so he also sees in 'In the Penal Colony' a possibility for an inversion of the meaning of language.

David Kishik, one of Agamben's translators, points out that the connection Agamben lays between the apparatus in Kafka's penal colony and language is also an important reference to Foucault's concept of *dispositif*, which is translated into English as 'apparatus'. In '*What is an Apparatus?*', Agamben gives an interpretation of this term in Foucault's work. Apparatuses are not evil in themselves but have been developed primarily to humanize people, to bring them happiness. Although they have degenerated into a means for subjecting people and controlling them, they also offer an important possibility for liberation from this.

The above interpretation of 'In the Penal Colony' does not completely exhaust its significance, according to Agamben: the essence of Kafka's story becomes clear primarily in the second half. When the officer has placed the condemned man under the apparatus to execute his sentence, he suddenly turns to the explorer. He confides in him that the punishment does not

22 Jessica Whyte, '"Its Silent Working Was a Delusion"'. In *The Work of Giorgio Agamben: Law, Literature, Life*, edited by Nicholas Heron, Justin Clemens and Alex Murray. (Edinburgh: Edinburgh University Press, 2008), 71.

23 DelaDurantaye, *Agamben*, 129.

24 Vivian Liska, 'Der Messias in Der Schriftmaschine. Gesetz Und Schrift in Giorgio Agambens Kafka-Lektüren'. *Trans. Internet-Zeitschrift für Kulturwissenschaften* 16 (2006).

have many supporters and that the new commandant of the penal colony is opposed to it. He begs the explorer to declare his support for the apparatus to the commandant, so that the latter will have no reason to dispose of it. But the explorer has already been filled with disgust at the sight of the apparatus and is looking for a way to show this, so he refuses to help. Although 'he was travelling with the sole purpose of observing and by no means altering other people's legal institutions', this affair tempted him too much.[25] When the officer hears that the explorer will not help him, the story takes an unexpected turn.

> 'Then, the time has come,' he said finally and suddenly looked at the traveller with shining eyes.[26]

The officer orders the condemned man released, who begins to laugh silently to himself. The officer then lies under the apparatus himself, but not before he has the explorer read the paper with the sentence that he places in the scriber. This text is decisive for Agamben's interpretation of the story. While the condemned man was given a precise order, i.e. 'Respect your superiors', the officer has sought a pure and simple order for himself: 'Be just'. And, Agamben argues, 'it is precisely when the apparatus tries to write this injunction that not only does it break apart, but it fails to perform its task' (IP, 116):

> 'The harrow was not writing, it was only jabbing … this was no exquisite torture … this was plain murder.' Thus on the officer's face there is no sign of the promised redemption: 'what the others had found in the machine the officer had not found.' (IP, 116)

Agamben sees in the officer a Messiah figure who has entered the command 'Be just', not because he has broken this command but as an instruction to destroy the apparatus. The officer is completely aware of this, as is apparent from the shining in his eyes when he says, 'Then the time has come'. Agamben declares: 'There can be no doubt: he inserts the instruction into the machine with the intention of destroying it' (IP, 117). But why does the machine fall apart when it has to engrave the order 'Be just'?

> The ultimate meaning of language – the tale now seems to say – is the injunction 'Be just'; and yet it is precisely the meaning of this injunction that the machine of language is absolutely incapable of getting us to understand. Or rather, it can do it only by ceasing to perform its penal function, only by shattering into pieces and turning from punisher

[25] Kafka, *Selected Stories*, 46.
[26] Ibid., 53.

> to murderer. In this way justice triumphs over justice, language over language. (IP, 117)

Justice demands the revocation and destruction of language and law.[27] That the officer does not find any redemption in the machine is because at that time there was nothing more to understand in language for him. Liska argues that the officer, as a Messiah figure, as a person who had come to abolish the law, apparently always knew the true meaning of language. Kafka's portrayal of the officer as a messianic figure is reinforced by the iron pick sticking out of his forehead and his look 'full of calm and conviction' when the apparatus falls apart. It is striking that, in Agamben's interpretation, it is precisely the sovereign who takes the role of the Messiah upon himself and that the inversion occurs in the extreme point of indistinguishability between the state of exception and the real state of exception, the meaning of language and the real meaning of language, the Messiah and the sovereign.[28]

Old times?

In his essay 'Law and Life', Rainer Maria Kiesow reflects on why Agamben does not refer to the story of the penal colony in *Homo Sacer*. Kiesow sees many elements of bare life in this story: the disappearance of the distinction between life and law, between accusation and judgement. However, Kiesow continues, in Kafka's story, bare life and the law that has gone astray, appear only as belonging to an old order: the time of the penal colony that has been coming to an end since the new commandant arrived.[29] The indistinguishability between law and life belongs, in Kiesow's view, to the past, such that 'In the Penal Colony' turns out to be Kafka's only story in which the law appears decipherable and this is also the only story in which Kafka describes 'the old time'. And it is this decipherability that leads irrevocably to the death of the one who deciphers it. In Kafka's other stories, which belong to the new time, the law remains indecipherable: Joseph K. finds only pornographic pictures in the books of law; Bucephalus leafs through the books of law. The law is no longer written on one's body. Kiesow sees this as a sign that the time of the *homo sacer*, of the old order, has been gone for a long time and that the law has already dissolved into a perfect nihilism. Agamben's claim that we are all

27 Liska, 'The Messiah before the Law', 168.

28 Ibid., 167.

29 Rainer Kiesow, 'Law and Life'. In *Politics, Metaphysics and Death. Essays on Giorgio Agamben's Homo Sacer*, edited by Andrew Norris. (Durham, NC: Duke University Press, 2005), 257.

potential *homini sacri* is an exaggeration from this point of view, because this only belonged to the old times.

Kiesow's interpretation can be read in two ways. It can be read first as a criticism of Agamben: i.e. Agamben uses Kafka selectively only to confirm his negative world view and does not cite any of Kafka's stories that give a different interpretation. But Kiesow himself seems to be using Agamben selectively and overlooks the possibilities Agamben describes in *Idea of Prose* with reference to Kafka's 'In the Penal Colony'. Another reading of Kiesow shows, however, that Agamben's philosophy has a positive message: the messianic age he describes has already dawned and signifies that the days of the *homo sacer* are coming to an end.

Nonetheless, there is still an important objection to Kiesow's interpretation, i.e. the fact that he has a completely different view of chronological time to Agamben. The latter's archaeology does not portray chronological, successive ages but only 'remnants' and the indistinguishability between the different eras. Agamben does not describe a chronological redemption; he only describes small doors through which the Messiah can enter, as we will see in the next chapter.

8

Strategies in Response to Time (1)

The original task of a genuine revolution, therefore, is never merely to 'change the world', but also – and above all – to 'change time'.

(Agamben, IH, 99)

Introduction

Just as our understanding of language traps us in a metaphysical world view and constitutes our political situation, so the same occurs with respect to our conception of time. Agamben sees a strong connection between law, messianism, language and time. 'The original task of a genuine revolution, therefore, is never merely to "change the world", but also – and above all – to "change time"' (IP, 99). Although messianism is mostly seen as a chronological 'end of time' that gives new meaning to law and language, Agamben shows that messianism also presents us with a new concept of time. Agamben sees in Kafka's stories and aphorisms on time various leads for developing a theory against the metaphysical, chronological time in favour of a 'now time', which offers a way out from how we are trapped by our view of chronological time.

Agamben sees an important task for art and tradition to 'change time'. Because of the changing role of art, it can no longer offer us an immediate experience, an experience of the moment, of the now. But Agamben does not only describes a certain Nihilism in art; he also searches for a perfect nihilism here. In the intransmissibility of content through form, he sees an important possibility or strategy that also emerges in Kafka's literary art. The latter's story 'Building the Great Wall of China' is an exquisite example of this.

The second problem lies in the intransmissibility of tradition and culture. Because of this intransmissibility, the human being is no longer connected with his past, which entails that his future also remains closed to him. This will be illustrated via Benjamin's image of a tradition that has fallen ill, which he sees reflected in Kafka's work, a view of Odradek as *Nachleben* and Kafka's story 'The City Coat of Arms' that offers important insights into the relation between time, transmissibility, language and the completion of metaphysics. The chapter hereafter will explore a new view of time that can be found in Kafka's work.

Time as chronological compulsion

No longer able to find the present

'Man is no longer able to find, between past and future, the space of present and gets lost in the linear time of history', Agamben argues in *The Man without Content* (111). This is also nicely illustrated in one of Kafka's short stories, 'He':[1]

> He has two antagonists: the first pushes him from behind, from his origin. The second blocks his road ahead. He struggles with both. Actually the first supports him in his struggle with the second, for the first wants to push him forward; and in the same way the second supports him in his struggle with the first; for the second of course forces him back. But it is only theoretically so. For it is not only the two protagonists who are there, but he himself as well and who really knows his intentions? However that may be, he has a dream that sometime in an unguarded moment – it would require, though, a night as dark as no night has ever been – he will spring out of the fighting line and be promoted, on account of his experience of such warfare, as judge over his struggling antagonists.[2]

In Agamben's view, our Western idea of time is understood in terms of moments and continuity. Aristotle defined time as a continuum consisting of passing points in which there is a 'before' and an 'after' (IH, 101). The moment itself is nothing more than a continuity of time, a pure limit that is both part of and introduces a distinction between, past and future. In the Christian view of time, time has an origin, a direction and an end: it moves from creation to the Day of Judgement. Although this is a completely different view from that of the ancient Greeks, the idea of a continuum of fleeting moments continues to exist (IH, 104). Our current idea of time is a based on this Christian view.

A culture with such an experience of time cannot have a true experience of the past or the present, according to Agamben. The human being is split between a being-in-time as an elusive stream of moments and a being-in-history, understood as the original dimension of the human being, a

[1] For an interpretation of this Kafka quote by Hannah Arendt and Arendt's influence on Agamben, see Liska (2008), 'Die Tradierbarkeit der Lücke in der Zeit'. Liska argues that Agamben's interpretation goes much further than Arendt's and that he does see a possibility for the main character to jump into the gulf between past and future.

[2] Kafka, 'He', 160–1.

diachronic reality and a synchronic structure that never coincide (IH, 109), a 'no more' and a 'not yet'.

This impossibility of the human being finding its place in the present coheres, in Agamben's view, with the metaphysical problem of transmissibility and with the division between form and content. Since antiquity, there have been two ways to experience the present and the past, to experience our history. The first is the transmissibility of tradition and culture; the second is art. Tradition has offered a certain continuity in time (experience of the past) and art a certain interruption of time (experience of the present). Due to the metaphysical divisions it has become impossible to just transmit content via a form without residue; both art and tradition have lost their function. This results, on the one hand, in the fact that the human being is caught between past and future, unable to find its place in history. On the other hand, art and tradition also offer another way out. But let us first look closer at Agamben's analysis of tradition and art and how they lost their function.

Tradition as continuity in time

In traditional societies, culture consists only in the living act of its transmission: there is no difference between what is transmitted and the transmission itself; there is no residue. But in non-traditional cultures, such as Western societies in which we live at this time, culture has lost its vital power. A split has occurred between the thing that is transmitted and the act of transmission. Agamben speaks of an 'accumulated treasure of ideas and precepts that constitute the separate object of transmission' in contrast to a complete coincidence between the thing transmitted and the act of transmission. Another characteristic of this metaphysical split is that the thing that is transmitted is valued more highly than the act of transmission (MWC, 107). Since transmission is the central characteristic of a tradition, this means a break in tradition and a discontinuity in our experience of time.

> Loss of tradition means that the past has lost its transmissibility and so long as no new way has been found to enter into a relation with it, it can only be the object of accumulation from now on. … For it is the transmissibility of culture that, by endowing culture with an immediately perceptible meaning and value, allows man to move freely toward the future without being hindered by the burden of the past. (MWC, 108)

But this break with tradition does not mean that the past no longer plays any role. On the contrary, tradition has, paradoxically, received extra importance.

With this loss of the transmissibility of culture, the human being finds himself caught, on the one hand, between 'a past that incessantly accumulates behind him and oppresses him with the multiplicity of its now-indecipherable contents and, on the other, a future that he does not yet possess and that does not throw any light on his struggle with the past' (MWC, 108). In the way Kafka describes the castle (with the obscurity of its decrees and the endless number of little offices), Agamben sees a good example of how the accumulated culture has lost its vital significance and oppresses the human being.

> Suspended in the void between old and new, past and future, man is projected into time as into something alien that incessantly eludes him and still drags him forward, but without allowing him to find his ground in it. (MWC, 108)

Agamben sees a parallel between the difficulty of finding one's place in history and in the present and Kafka's journal entry on the travellers who have been involved in a train accident in a tunnel (MWC, 112):

> Travelers in a train that has met with an accident in a tunnel and this at a place where the lights of the beginning can no longer be seen and the light of the end is so very small a glimmer that the gaze must continually search for it and is always losing it again and, furthermore, it is not even certain whether it is the beginning or the end of the tunnel.[3]

Agamben sees in Benjamin's angel of history the same image of the human being who has lost his relationship with the past and no longer finds himself in the future either. Benjamin, a great lover of the artist Klee, describes one of the latter's paintings, *Angelus Novus*, in which he sees an angel whose eyes are staring, mouth open, wings spread. This, Benjamin argues, is what the angel of history must look like. The angel of history is directed to the past and what he sees is a major catastrophe that heaps wreckage upon wreckage. 'The angel would like to stay, awaken the dead and make whole what has been smashed. But a storm is blowing from Paradise and has caught in his wings; it is so strong that the angel can no longer close them. This storm drives him irresistibly into the future, to which his back is turned'.[4] This image by Benjamin has strong affinities with Kafka's description of the 'he' figure, torn apart between two opponents, pushing him from behind and from the front without his being able to escape. Using this image by Kafka and Benjamin's 'angel of history', Agamben describes the catastrophe that

[3] Kafka, *Diaries*, 15.
[4] Benjamin, *Selected Writings 4*, 392.

results from our view of historical time, where we are unable to find our place in history and in the present.

Art as the interruption of time

Analogous to his description of the loss of tradition and transmissibility as a means to find our ground of existence in time, Agamben also describes a loss with respect to art. He describes how, halfway through the seventeenth century, a division occurred in art between form and content, between artist and viewer and between good taste and bad taste, art and kitsch. For the ancient Greeks, art had the task of bringing about an immediate experience of the divine, which led either to ecstasy or to horror. In this, art was very close to life and the experience of the 'self'. At present, following Kant, a trend has taken place in which the ecstasy is removed from art and, instead, one attempts to form an objective judgement of what beauty is and is not, what true art is and what is kitsch. Even if the artist himself still experiences this ecstasy in the present time, it remains the task of the viewers to assume an attitude of distance with respect to art. Looking at a work of art, according to Agamben, is no longer ecstasy but a possibility for the viewer to display his good taste and aesthetic judgement. The content and the form of art are no longer transmitted without residue directly to the viewer. Rather, the viewer goes in search of the content behind the form, which nonetheless continually escapes him. 'Every time aesthetic judgment attempts to determine what the beautiful is, it holds in its hands not the beautiful but its shadow, as though its true object were not so much what art is but what it is not: not art but non-art' (MWC, 42). Following Hegel, Agamben describes a self-annihilation of art, a nihilism in art. But here as well he sees a possibility for perfect nihilism.

Kafka's description of perfect nihilism as the ground on which we live, of the free life in the shadow of the Great Wall of China, the mighty paw of transmissibility, Odradek's *Nachleben*, the closed fist in the city coat of arms, the lightness of the bucket rider and the Messiah who comes the day after offer us important strategies to overturn our current concept of time as a chronological compulsion.

Kafka's art: Perfect nihilism as the ground of our existence

How is Kafka's art, his literature, related to this original task of art, which has lost its function? Agamben describes the new task of art via an angel of art, inspired by Dürer's engraving *Melancholia*. This engraving depicts, in Agamben's view, the loss of art and shows an inversion of Benjamin's angel of history.

Dürer's engraving shows an angel staring straight ahead, unmoving and melancholic. Lying next to the angel are the tools for an active life: a grindstone, nails, a hammer, a set square, pincers and a saw. These objects have lost their significance, their content. The angel of art is melancholic because he sees that the world has become alienated from him and he has accepted this; it is the nostalgia of a reality that he can possess only by making it unreal; transcendence cannot be captured in a form.

The melancholia of this angel, its passivity, shows a new task of art, one Kafka practised according to Agamben. A task that will inverse the horrified angel of history. The work of art has the task of taking up the tradition before it became divided, albeit in a radically different way, i.e. not by searching for the content behind the form but by making the form itself central, in the same way as only the 'indefatigable demystifying action of the land surveyor K. ensures for Count West-West's castle the sole appearance of reality it can lay claim to' (MWC, 111). In the same way, the work of art ensures the survival of the accumulated culture: on the one hand, it offers the accumulated past as a source of aesthetic enjoyment in museums and, on the other, this enjoyment is possible only through the alienation that arises because its meaning has been removed (MWC, 111). 'Content is sacrificed to the work of art. The thing to be transmitted is sacrificed to the act of transmission.'[5]

There is an hourglass behind the angel, but the angel seems to be in a kind of atemporal dimension, a frozen history, an interval between past and future. Precisely in this interval, according to Agamben, not only lies a loss, but also an immanent opening. 'Even though tragedy lies in this interval, the interval itself cannot be totally tragic. As revelatory appearance, as truth, this space returns to us our essential solidarity and common ground'.[6] Dürer's melancholic angel of art is also the angel who represents a messianic pause in time, a possibility of escaping from historicity, an angel who brings redemption for the past (MWC, 110). Art is both mystery and revelation or, as in Baudelaire's metaphor, a flash of lightning: 'a flash … then night!' (cited in MWC, 106).

> Art succeeds … in transforming man's inability to exit his historical status, perennially suspended in the inter-world between old and new, past and future, into the very space in which he can take the original

[5] DelaDurantaye, *Agamben*, 48.

[6] Daniel Morris, 'Life, or Something Like It. The Philosophical Chiaroscuro of Giorgio Agamben'. *Bookforum*, Summer 2004 (2004).

> measure of his dwelling in the present and recover each time the meaning of his action. (MWC, 114)

A reaction in art to this impossibility of the human being to find himself in time is depicted in the Greek tragedies 'by the figure of a guilty innocent, a tragic hero who, in all his greatness and misery, expresses the precious interest in human action in the interval between that which no longer is and what is not yet.' And, according to Agamben, Kafka is the author *par excellence* who has taken this task of art concerning time upon himself, as was also illustrated in Kafka's fragment cited above about two opponents that pushed at him from the future and from the past.[7] Against the 'nullified present of the metaphysical tradition', Agamben places 'a present which is not a transition, but in which time stands still and has come to a stop' (IH, 102). An example of this and a possibility to make of this the ground of our existence, can be found in Kafka's story 'Building the Great Wall of China'.

A free life in the shadow of the Great Wall of China

Beda Allemann's interpretation of Kafka's story 'Building the Great Wall of China' has greatly influenced Agamben's analysis of the understanding of history and time in Kafka's work. Agamben reads it as an illustration of how the impossibility of finding one's ground of existence in historical time can be the ground itself on which we live, which is the new task of art.

In Kafka's story, there is a first person narrator who is a researcher,[8] a history scholar. But, according to Alleman, it is characteristic of Kafka's work that the soundness of the research does not lead to a satisfactory theory. To the contrary, it leads to the recognition of the entire incomprehensibility of what one is attempting to understand through the precise recording of facts and a rigorous study of the information. 'In Kafka's work, the characters engaged in research are characterised by the fact that, long before they reach any results, they have returned to their premises'.[9]

The scholar, a man from the south of China, attempts to understand the logic behind the fact that, rather than being built in its entirety all at once, the Chinese Wall was built at different places in the country. It was only over the course of time that completely separate sections should become joined.

[7] Cited in the section on 'Time as Chronological Compulsion'.

[8] Just as in Kafka's stories 'The Village Schoolmaster', 'Researches of a Dog' and 'A Report to an Academy'.

[9] Beda Allemann, 'Kafka Et L'histoire'. In *L'endurance De La Pensée: Pour Saluer Jean Beaufret.*, edited by R. Char. (Paris: Plon, 1968), 79.

The scholar wants to understand the intentions of the emperor who ordered the wall to be built.

One problem lies in the size of the empire: its enormity prevented news and reports from the imperial palace in Peking from reaching the villages in the south. And if reports did reach the south, they were contradictory. 'We certainly heard a good deal, but we could not take anything from this abundance'.[10] This resulted in the inhabitants in the south not having any real idea of the historical developments that were occurring:

> Hopelessly and hopefully, our people view the emperor. They do not know which emperor is reigning and there is even doubt about the name of the dynasty. … In our villages, long-dead emperors are set up on thrones and one who lives on only in songs has recently issued a decree that the priest reads aloud in front of the altar. Battles from our most ancient history are just now being fought and with glowing cheeks your neighbour bursts into your house with the news. … If once, once in a lifetime, an imperial official touring the provinces accidentally comes into our village, makes certain demands in the name of the ruler … a smile flickers across all our faces, each man looks furtively to the next and bends down to the children so as not to be observed by the official. What, you think, he is speaking about a dead man like someone who is alive, this emperor died a long time ago, the dynasty was wiped out, the official is making fun of us, but we will act as if we did not notice, so as not to hurt his feelings.[11]

Just as in the quote above on the two opponents, the Chinese in the south are not able to find a place for themselves in the history of the succession of imperial dynasties. But that does not mean that history is less real for them: with glowing cheeks, they tell one another news about something that probably happened long ago.[12] But although the quote primarily describes a struggle, 'Building the Great Wall of China' is in many respects a joyful narrative. Strangely enough, in their lack of historicity the villagers find a basis, a unity.

> 'Anyone intent on concluding from such phenomena that we basically have no emperor at all would not be far from the truth', the narrator argues, 'Now, the result of such opinions is, to a certain extent, a free, ungoverned life.'[13]

[10] Kafka, *Selected Stories*, 119.
[11] Kafka, *Selected Stories*, 120–1.
[12] Allemann, *Kafka*, 81.
[13] Kafka, *Selected Stories*, 122.

That the central power of the emperor had no actual significance for the inhabitants of the province resulted in a life that is lived in a kind of singular freedom.[14]

The narrator describes a certain contradictory tendency in the Chinese in the south: on the one hand, they do not succeed in embracing 'the empire obediently, in all its liveliness and presence, raising it from its submersion in Peking' and, on the other, they do not desire anything other than 'just for once to feel this connection and drown in it'.[15] But, the narrator states, 'it is all the more striking that precisely this weakness appears to be one of the most important means of unifying our people; indeed, if one may be so forward as to employ such an expression, it is the very ground on which we live'.[16]

> If the Chinese in the south are incapable of establishing immediate, real and present relationships with their supreme master, the emperor, so that they can take possession of their own present, this is nothing more than a reflection of the fundamental constitution of human existence.... Actually, for Kafka, human existence is characterized as a whole by a common fundamental trait: it is incapable of taking possession of its own historical presuppositions. That is why it is forced to be installed in specific interregnum.[17]

The Chinese in the south can remain in a gap in history. All the historical research of the narrator has shown is that it does not make any sense at all to look for a historical motivation behind the beginning of the construction of the Wall.[18] This event was, on the one hand, a historical event and, on the other, it shows the completely evasive, if not improbable, historical character of the Wall.[19] With this story, Kafka shows that, for him, history is an existing history and, at the same time, a nothing.

Hence, the new task of art, the art Kafka is practicing according to Agamben, is to establish a new relationship with time, past the metaphysical conception of time as continuous fleeing moments. A concept of time in which the inability to find our place in history is the ground we live on. History and time are not a chronological compulsion, but a small door that leaps into time. But then what does the new task of tradition look like?

14 Allemann, *Kafka*, 77.
15 Kafka, *Selected Stories*, 122–3.
16 Ibid., 123.
17 Allemann, *Kafka*, 84.
18 Ibid., 77–9.
19 Ibid., 81.

The mighty paw of transmissibility

Agamben describes tradition as a piling up of things that have lost their meaning, instead of a natural transmission of meaning. In Benjamin's interpretation of Kafka, he finds a clue for how this burden can be removed from our backs. According to Benjamin, Kafka's work describes a tradition that has fallen ill.[20] Agamben points out that according to Benjamin, the original meaning of tradition is on the one hand transmissibility and on the other betrayal. Something is lost, disfigured in transmission (PO, 105). According to Benjamin:

> Kafka eavesdropped on tradition. ... The main reason why this eavesdropping demands such effort is that only the most indistinct sounds reach the listener. There is no doctrine that one could learn and no knowledge that one could preserve.[21]

Benjamin draws an analogy with two Jewish concepts concerning the law: Haggadah and Halakah. The latter is the letter of the law, the truth, the doctrine. Haggadah, on the other hand, is the spirit of the law, the possibility of transmission, the stories and anecdotes about the Talmud, which are intended to explain and confirm Halakah. According to Benjamin, wisdom is the epic side of the truth and is found in the Haggadah rather than in the Halakah. This makes wisdom a property of tradition. But it is precisely this Haggadic consistency of the truth that has been lost in the metaphysical emphasis on true nature: tradition has become sick.

Most authors who have faced this problem between Haggadah and Halakah responded by letting go of tradition for the sake of truth. Kafka's genius lies, according to Benjamin, in his doing precisely the opposite: he sacrificed the truth for its transmissability. And the strength of this is that the Haggadah is no longer related to a Halakah. As Agamben puts it: 'In Kafka the Law rebels against itself so that the stories of the Talmud are vying for transmission of the Law' (ELJ, 2009).

That is why Kafka's parables evade any interpretation, as different authors have remarked. [22] According to Benjamin, Kafka is no longer concerned about truth, but about rumours about true things and foolishness (a kind of theology passed on in whispers on matters that have fallen into disuse and discredit). In Benjamin's words:

[20] Benjamin and Scholem, *Correspondence*, 225.

[21] Ibid., 224.

[22] Benjamin, *Selected Writings*; Hamacher, 'The Gesture in the Name'; Theodor Adorno, 'Notes on Kafka'. In *Prisms* (Cambridge: MIT Press, 1983).

> Kafka's writings are by their nature parables. But that is their misery and their beauty, that they had to become *more* than parables. They do not modestly lie at the feet of doctrine, as Haggadah lies at the feet of Halakah. When they have crouched down, they unexpectedly raise a mighty paw against it.[23]

Liska points out that Agamben goes a step further in his interpretation than Benjamin. If Benjamin speaks about 'raising a powerful paw against it', Agamben inclines more to a total removal of Halakah and Haggadah.[24]

In his essay written on the occasion of the tenth anniversary of Kafka's death, Benjamin explores this relationship with the past and the burden of culture without significance more closely. He quotes three of Kafka's characters who have liberated themselves from it, who have sacrificed the truth for the sake of transmissibility. These are: the students who do not write, the horse Bucephalus, who has survived his mythical rider Alexander the Great and Sancho Panza, who has succeeded in distracting his knight and having him walk in front of him. 'Whether it is a man or a horse is no longer so important', Benjamin concludes, 'if only the burden is taken off the back.'[25]

One of the new tasks of tradition, a strategy against time as compulsion, is to sacrifice truth for the sake of transmissibility, as Kafka did according to Benjamin. Then the accumulated culture will be removed from our back. The second aspect of this strategy, as Odradek's *Nachleben* shows, is that it inverses chronological time into a history that is not chronological, but is based on the remnant.

Odradek's *Nachleben*

In one of his earlier texts, Benjamin gave another interpretation of Kafka's Haggadah where he rejects a chronological development of the law from a lawless state of nature to a world of law. The state of nature leaves a residue in the present world of law, Benjamin claims. Kafka depicts this by stating that the law is described in books but these books are secret. His parables show the residue of the previous world in the law, in Halakah. Kafka's

[23] Benjamin and Scholem, *Correspondence*, 225.

[24] Vivian Liska, 'Als Ob Nicht. Messianismus in Giorgio Agambens Kafka-Lektüren'. In *Die Gouvernementale Maschine. Zur Politischen Philosophi Giorgio Agambens*, edited by J. Böckelmann and F. Meier (Münster: Unrast-verlag, 2007), 75–90.

[25] Benjamin, *Selected Writings 2.2*, 816.

parables are the missing Haggadah for the Halakah that has been permeated by this previous world.[26]

Agamben also describes Kafka's stories as a revival of the prehistoric depths of the world that enter into history via a contradictory gesture (IH, 143): a return to the new. For Agamben, tradition is inseparably bound up with *Nachleben*, a term that he borrows from Warburg and that was also of great significance for Benjamin. *Nachleben* is a difficult term to translate: it is not so much life after (*nach*) this life as it is continuing life in this world; it can also be translated as survival.[27] But it not simply survival; it is survival beyond its meaning: a life after itself (see also Chapter 4 on Odradek).

Agamben sees in Odradek an example of *Nachleben* in the emblematic form that had so much significance in traditional society but gives an uncanny feeling in present society (S, 144). Odradek symbolizes an example of a creature that doesn't belong to chronological time, a residue behind meaning.

The closed fist in the city coat of arms

Different lines of Agamben's interpretation of Kafka's work converge in his idea of tradition and transmissibility. First is his view of the law as being in force without significance, which is now described in terms of Haggadah and Halakah, where law is released from any claim of transcendence.

Second is Agamben's view of language as a pure possibility of communication, released from any focus on the content of the communication. The transmission of the impossibility of transmissability is that which constitutes human language as such (PO, 105). Agamben refers to another of Kafka's stories, 'The City Coat of Arms', that depicts this relation between language and tradition nicely. The story begins with the assertion that everything was quite well arranged in the beginning when construction on the Tower of Babel started, but that changed quickly:

> So long as there are men on the earth there will be also the irresistible desire to complete the building. That being so, however, one needs to have no anxiety about the future; on the contrary, human knowledge is increasing, the art of building has made progress and will make further progress, a piece of work which takes us a year may perhaps be done in half the time in another hundred years and better done, too, more

[26] Hanssen, *Walter Benjamin*, 138.

[27] DelaDurantaye, *Agamben*, 70.

> enduringly. So why exert oneself to the extreme limit of one's present powers? There would be some sense in doing that only if it were likely that the tower could be completed in one generation. But that is beyond all hope. It is far more likely that the next generation with their perfect knowledge will find the work of their predecessors bad and tear down what has been built so as to begin anew. Such thoughts paralysed people's powers and so they troubled less about the tower than the construction of a city for the workmen. … To this must be added that the second or third generation had already recognized the senselesness of building a heaven-reaching tower; but by that time everybody was too deeply involved to leave the city.
>
> All the legends and songs that came to birth in that city are filled with longing for a prophesied day when the city would be destroyed by five successive blows from a gigantic fist. It is for that reason too that the city has a closed fist on its coat of arms.[28]

In this symbol of the city coat of arms with the closed fist – of which it is said that it would complete tradition – Agamben sees the transmission of the unrevealed. This closed fist does not transmit a transcendent meaning, but a being-thus and it is precisely on this transmission that Agamben's new concept of language is based (PO, 105).

The third line that converges with the above two in Agamben's view of tradition and transmissibility is his view of messianic time against chronological time. 'The cancellation of the law and of the reference structures of language correspond to the cancellation of the distinction between chronological time and redeemed time.'[29] The final chapter will discuss this new view of time.

[28] Kafka, *Complete Stories*, 433–4.
[29] Liska, 'Als Ob Nicht', 77.

9

Strategies in Response to Time (2)

'Every instant can be the little door through which the Messiah enters.'
(Walter Benjamin, cited in TL, 7)

Introduction

In the previous chapter, we met with two aspects of Agamben's new concept of time: a new task for art and one for tradition that makes our inability to find our place between past and future the very ground on which to live and that by doing so sacrifices truth for transmissability. In this chapter, we will further explore Agamben's new concept of time which he bases on Kafka's stories, such as his story of the bucket rider. Agamben indicates an important contradictory symmetry between Nietzsche's idea of eternal return and Kafka's bucket rider. Secondly, Kafka's aphorisms about the coming of the Messiah play an especially important role in Agamben's new concept of time.

The lightness of the bucket rider

In one of the scenes from Nietzsche's *Thus Spoke Zarathustra*, the prophet Zarathustra climbs a mountain via a rocky, lonely path. On his shoulders he carries a creature as heavy as lead, of paralyzing weight, which he calls 'The Spirit of Gravity'. This is his archenemy, a creature that is half dwarf, half mole and in which Agamben sees a Kafkaesque creature (QGK, 41).[1] While Zarathustra struggles to climb higher up the mountain, the Spirit of Gravity whispers derisively in his ear: 'O Zarathustra … you philosopher's stone! You threw yourself up high, but every stone that is thrown must fall.'[2] This Spirit of Gravity turns the human being into a camel, too heavily laden with things that are not his own and making the things that could be his own also (too)

[1] Friedrich Nietzsche, *Thus Spoke Zarathustra: A Book for All and None*. Trans. Walter Kaufmann. (New York: Random House) 1995, 156.

[2] Ibid., 151.

heavy to bear.[3] Every attempt to exalt oneself will end in a fall, according to the Spirit of Gravity.

Dejected, the prophet climbs on, but when they arrive at a gate he confronts the Spirit of Gravity with the idea of 'the greatest gravity'. The inscription above the gate reads 'moment' and, according to Zarathustra, two unending paths converge here: the past and the present. The prophet asks: 'Are not all things knotted together so firmly that this moment draws after it *all* that is to come? *Therefore – itself too*?' (italics added).[4] 'Moment' is not a fixed point in time, but a stream that drags everything with it and in this is also itself a repetition. This dialogue between Zarathustra and the Spirit of Gravity echoes Nietzsche's idea of eternal return, which he himself called an idea of the greatest gravity. This idea contains the following thought experiment: if one is told that one would have to live his life endlessly over again and in precisely the same way as one has lived it until now, how would one respond?

> Would you not throw yourself down and gnash your teeth and curse the demon who spoke thus? Or did you once experience a tremendous moment when you would have answered him, 'You are a god and never have I heard anything more godly'.[5]

This idea raises the question of whether one could live without the consoling notion of transcendence, in the here and now, only in this world and in this life. This notion of the abandonment of transcendence also echoes Nietzsche's famous statement that God is dead.[6] Nihilism reaches its most extreme form in Nietzsche's idea of eternal return, but it is precisely for this reason that it enters an area in which it becomes possible to inverse it (MWC, 89–90/134).

Can one live in the moment, in the *kairos*, as opposed to living in chronological time? Although the dwarf grumbles that time is a circle, this is not the same as the eternal return and the image of the snake that bites its own tail is destroyed a few scenes further on when Zarathustra and the dwarf find a shepherd who is screaming for help. A snake had crawled into the shepherd's mouth while he was asleep and he is trying in vain to pull it out. 'Bite! Bite its head off! Bite!' Zarathustra shouts at him. When he does, the shepherd is

3 Ibid., 188.

4 Ibid., 153; 158.

5 Friedrich Nietzsche, *The Gay Science: With a Prelude in Rhymes and an Appendix of Songs*. Trans. Walter Kaufmann (Vintage Books, 1974), 273.

6 DelaDurantaye, *Agamben*, 318–19.

able to rid himself of this snake and becomes 'radiant'.[7] At that moment the burden of eternal return is surpassed in a life in the moment.

The moment that drags past and future and itself after it abolishes the relation between moment and history.

> At the point where the shepherd bites off the head of the snake that has crawled into his throat, the weight is converted into the most exalted flight. … Zarathustra substantially accepts the judgment of the dwarf ('every stone that is thrown must – fall back down again'), but astutely transforms it into its opposite: the stone that eternally falls back down again is the lightest thing of all. (QGK, 41)

Although Agamben is considerably more ambivalent in his later work towards Nietzsche's idea of eternal return (in particular because, in Agamben's view, Nietzsche did not pay enough attention to the irreparable),[8] in his earlier work he does acknowledge an important form of potentiality, of possibility, in the notion of eternal return, or better, in an adjusted version of the eternal return. In the idea of eternal return, act and passivity converge; time comes to a standstill and the subject is thrown completely back on to itself to make this the ground of its being (ER, 16).

Agamben sees a contradictory symmetry in Nietzsche's story with Kafka's story of the bucket rider. The main character in this story does not have any money to buy coal during a freezing cold winter. He decides to go to the coal dealer with a bucket to see if he will sell him any on credit:

> But once downstairs my bucket ascends, superbly, superbly; camels humbly squatting on the ground do not rise with more dignity, shaking themselves under the sticks of their drivers. Through the hard-frozen streets we go at a regular canter; often I am upraised as high as the first storey of a house; never do I sink as low as the house doors. And at last I float at an extraordinary height above the vaulted cellar of the dealer. … 'Coal dealer!' I cry in a voice burned hollow by the frost and muffled in the cloud made by my breath, 'please, coal dealer, give me a little coal. My bucket is so light that I can ride on it. Be kind. When I can I'll pay you'.[9]

While the Spirit of Gravity oppresses Zarathustra in Nietzsche's story and he seeks lightness for his falling stone, the bucket rider in Kafka's story wants to get a hold of some weight and be able to descend to earth: 'It is an excess

7 Nietzsche, *Zarathustra*, 155; 159.

8 Leland DelaDurantaye, 'Agamben's Potential'. *diacritics* 30, no. 2 (2000), 15–16.

9 Kafka, *Complete Stories*, 413.

of light, a lack of weight that borders on misery, that, against every force of gravity, lifts up the rider' (QGK, 41). And, although the coal dealer almost seems to give in to the pleadings of the bucket rider, his wife chases him away. The bucket rider's light mount is easily brushed aside by the woman's apron. And thus, the bucket rider disappears from sight, floating towards the freezing cold regions of the Ice Mountains and is never seen again.

If Zarathustra finds inversion in eternal return, the fate of the bucket rider is the opposite:

> His fate is not the eternal return, but the lightness of a feather that the wind forever carries away, 'to never meet again.' True lightness – he seems to be saying – is not the eternal return, but never to return. … (His opposite is the hunter Gracchus, who was unable to break free from the earth and whose boat is doomed to sail forever on the earthly waters, driven by the wind "that blows in the lower regions of death"). Instead, the knight finds his peace in the realm of the Ice Mountains. A draft of an epilogue is shown to us as he, dismounted from his horse, wanders in the cold carrying his mount on his shoulders. This high, lightness no longer serves any function: so much so that he carries it on his back. (QGK, 42)

We see an image returning here that is similar to Benjamin's, in which Kafka's characters succeed in removing the burden from their back or in which the burden no longer has any weight.[10] The Italian novelist Italo Calvino takes over this image of lightness as showing us a possibility for a new age. Shortly before his death, he gave a lecture on 'Lightness'[11] in which Kafka's story of the bucket rider played an important role. For Calvino, lightness is not frivolity but a way to show that the world, instead of consisting of impenetrable material, consists of innumerable tiny particles that are light, moving and bearers of information. Calvino describes two tendencies in literature: lightness and heaviness. Although Kafka seems to fall at first under the category of 'heaviness', Calvino sees many 'light' elements. He compares Kafka's bucket rider to an unexpected, light jump that raises one above the heaviness of the world.[12]

[10] Benjamin *Selected Writings 2.2*, 816.

[11] The theme of lightness plays an important role in Calvino's work and is also one of the themes of the journal on which Calvino worked between 1974 and 1976, together with Claudio Rugafiori and Giorgio Agamben, but which was never published. The final discussion between Calvino and Agamben was on lightness (DelaDurantaye, *Agamben*, 318).

[12] Italo Calvino, *Six Memos for the Next Millennium* (Cambridge: Harvard University Press, 1988), 22.

> But the idea of an empty bucket raising you above the level where one finds both the help and the egoism of others; the empty bucket, symbol of privation and desire and seeking, raising you to the point at which a humble request can no longer be satisfied – all this opens the road to endless reflection. … Thus, astride our bucket, we shall face the new millennium, without hoping to find anything more in it than what we ourselves are able to bring to it. Lightness, for example, whose virtues I have tried to illustrate here.[13]

And thus lightness and heaviness are closely connected. If the conversion from heaviness into a perfect nihilism is connected with eternal return, lightness is connected in a perfect nihilism with never returning again: life in *kairos*, instead of in linear time. 'Every instant can be the little door through which the Messiah enters.'[14]

The Messiah who comes the day after his arrival

What Agamben finds in Kafka's work is a new view of history and a new view of time. Both are closely connected with Kafka's aphorisms on the coming of the Messiah. Although he devotes only a few sentences to this, they play an important role in Agamben's work and his view of time.

Kafka's day of judgement as a *Kairos*

What ways out does Agamben see from our view of time as a constantly fleeting continuum of moments? A first attempt to make this time inoperative was already formulated in Greek antiquity by the Stoics in response to Aristotle's view of time. Against *chronos*, continuous time, they placed *kairos*. This is more than only a moment; it is a possibility that passes by and people have to seize on that moment. It is both within and outside our control, the abrupt and sudden conjunction where decision seizes the opportunity and life is fulfilled for a moment (IH, 111). This is also a moment of happiness and, as is well known, moments of happiness are characterized by an absence of quantifiable time. Agamben proposes a kairological view of history against a chronological view.

This kairology is precisely what he finds in Kafka's work and in the interpretations of Kafka by Allemann and Benjamin. What Kafka proposes is not

[13] Ibid., 28–9.
[14] Benjamin, cited in TL, 7.

a linear view of history but a 'state of history' that is not directed to the past, nor to the future, but only to the present. The strongest expression of this, perhaps, is found in his aphorisms on the coming of the Messiah and the Day of Judgement. As discussed earlier (Chapter 1), Kafka has an unorthodox view of the Day of Judgement. This day is not at the end of time, but is constantly taking place:

> Only our concept of Time makes it possible for us to call the day of the Last Judgment by that name; in reality it is a summary court in perpetual session [*Standrecht*].[15]

Kafka's Day of Judgement is a *Kairos.* This Day of Judgement is our historical condition, our state of history and not the continuum of fleeing moments. In the state of history, which is a messianic time, everything appears in the messianic 'now' and this is also the significance of the story about the train accident in the tunnel in which 'it is not even certain whether it is the beginning or the end of the tunnel.'[16] A similar idea can also be found in Nietzsche's idea of eternal return (TL, 9), or in the following aphorism by Kafka:

> The decisive moment in human evolution is perpetual. That is why the revolutionary spiritual movements that declare all former things worthless are in the right, for nothing has yet happened.[17]

Those who want to understand the state of history in Kafka's work must abandon a linear idea of history that leads us through moments to a final goal that lies in the future. As Kafka claims: 'There is a goal, but no path; what we call the path is only wavering.'[18] According to Agamben, 'The goal is inaccessible not because it is too far in the future but because it is present here in front of us' and we hesitate to acknowledge that (MWC, 133). The *kairos* is a moment we should seize when it passes by; it is not about an end to which history is headed and that we must reach. It is the moment we must appropriate when it is present. Redemption is not something that lies in the future, but something that can be appropriated at every moment.

According to Agamben, what we find in Kafka is an inversion of Benjamin's image of the angel of history:

> The angel has already arrived in Paradise – in fact he was there from the start and the storm and his subsequent flight along the linear time of

15 Kafka, 'Reflections', 287.
16 Kafka, *Octavo Notebooks*, 15.
17 Ibid., 16.
18 Kafka, 'Reflections', 283. Kishik points out that the Greek translation of euphoric aporia both means a 'felicitous way' and 'lack of way' (69).

> progress are nothing but an illusion he creates in the attempt to falsify his knowledge and to transform his perennial condition into an aim still to be attained. ... Kafka replaces the idea of a history infinitely unfolding along an empty, linear time (this is the history that compels the Angelus Novus to his unstoppable run) with the paradoxical image of a state of history in which the fundamental event of the human condition is perpetually taking place; the continuum of linear time is interrupted, but does not create an opening beyond itself. (MWC, 112-13)

Kafka replaces Benjamin's angel of history by the perfect nihilism of a state of history, in which the impossibility of grasping time is the human being's actual ground.

Messianic time and the coming of the Messiah

Kafka's aphorisms on the coming of the Messiah constitute another important source for understanding Kafka's new view of time and history. Before I will explore this source, we should first look at Agamben's view of messianic time.

Agamben holds that the traditional messianic view of time consists of a division: the time since creation until the Apocalypse and the time that dawns after the Apocalypse.[19] But, Agamben argues, there is a third time that dawns with the coming of the Messiah. The Messiah is often confused with the Apocalypse, but, according to Agamben, the Messiah indicates a different time, the messianic time. How can this messianic time best be understood, if not linearly? Agamben finds a possibility for viewing the messianic time in the work of the French linguist Gustave Guillaume. The latter argued that there is a large gap between the way in which we represent time and the way in which we experience it (TL, 4). Guillaume calls the mechanism by which we attempt to bridge this gap 'operational time'. If we speak about time, the mind needs a moment to link the experience of time to the available chronological representation.

Two things in this view are important for Agamben. Firstly, the time we experience can never coincide with the time we can represent. Secondly, there is a third time; this is not an additional time but a time that makes the

[19] In *Nudities*, Agamben describes how salvation precedes creation. The name of the Messiah was created before the world. God created the angels to maintain the work of creation and prophets for the work of salvations. According to a *hadith*, when God created the angels, they raised their heads and asked: 'Lord, who are you with?' He responded: 'I am with those who are victims of injustice until their rights are restored.' (N, 2–3).

other times inoperative. Agamben calls this 'messianic time' and describes it as:

> The time we need in order to accomplish, to bring to an end our representation of time. It is neither the time – representable but unthinkable – of chronological time, nor the instant – equally unthinkable – of its end. Nor is it a segment cut off from chronological time, a segment that goes from the resurrection up to the end of time. It is, rather, the operational time that drives chronological time and transforms it from within; it is the time it takes us to bring time to an end – in this sense: *the time which is left to us.* (TL, 5)

The time that remains to us is the time that we are. One danger is that this messianic time is viewed either as a fulfilment that adds something to complete our present time or as a supplement that adds something without completing it. What it concerns, according to Agamben, is a *parousia*, a 'being alongside itself', a type of concept we also saw in the paradigm and the parable. 'The messianic presence lies beside itself, because, without ever coinciding with a chronological instant and without adding to it, nevertheless it grasps and fulfills it' (TL, 7). The messianic time is neither the fulfilled nor the unfulfilled time, neither the past nor the future, but their inversion. The past becomes unfulfilled and the present, the unfulfilled, reaches a kind of perfection (TL, 9). Linear time is interrupted but creates no opening beyond itself. Historical time is not simply annulled, but messianic time is not simply homogeneous with history either.[20] That is also why Kafka states that the Messiah does not come on the last day but on the last day of all.

> The Messiah will come only when he is no longer necessary, he will come only one day after his arrival, he will not come on the last day, but on the last day of all.[21]

Only if we let go of the idea of historical time, Allemann states, can the Messiah come.[22] Kafka's Messiah comes only when there is nothing left to say. His gestures are no longer a prophecy nor a memory, revival or proclamation (IM, 116). Another, overlapping image of the coming of the Messiah, described by Benjamin, is that he has already come but we have not noticed it. Just as the *kairos* can pass us by without our seeing it because we are waiting for redemption at the end of time, so the Messiah can also pass us by without our noticing.

20 Mills, 'Playing with Law', 21.
21 Kafka, *Octavo Notebooks*, 28.
22 Alleman, 'Kafka', 88.

James Martel finds this theme present to a large extent in Kafka's work, primarily in *The Castle*, in which K. sees an impressive sledge parked beside a bar and waits by it in the hope that it belongs to Klamm so he can finally meet him.[23] While he waits for Klamm, however, a handsome young man appears in the bright light of the bar. He invites K. to go with him, but K. refuses: 'I am waiting for someone.' The man continues to press him, but K. answers: 'But then I'll miss the person I'm waiting for.' The man responds: 'You'll miss him whether you wait or you go.'[24]

Catherine Mills argues that, for Agamben, messianic time is not a chronological difference but an ontological difference that can appear at any moment.[25] It is a 'now' time. Agamben remarked in 'The Messiah and the Sovereign' that, according to writings by the Sanhedrin, the world would exist for six thousand years: 'two thousand in chaos, two thousand under the Law, two thousand during the messianic time.' But, we read further on, the time under the law has passed and the Messiah still has not come (PO, 168). Or we did not notice his coming because we have been trapped in chronological time. The reason why this has gone by unnoticed is because the Messiah does not bring the expected 'end of time':

> The Messiah has already arrived, the messianic event has already occurred, but its presence contains within itself another time, which stretches its promise not in order to defer it, but, on the contrary, to make it graspable, that it may be grasped. And this is why, in Walter Benjamin's words, every instant can be the little door through which the Messiah enters. (TL, 7)

[23] James Martel, 'The Messiah Who Comes and Goes: Franz Kafka on Redemption, Conspiracy and Community'. *Theory & Event* 12, no. 3 (2009).

[24] Kafka, *Castle*, 105.

[25] Mills, 'Playing with Law', 21.

Conclusion: Finding Freedom Beyond Subordination

Beyond the 'anguish of a guilty man before the inscrutable power', beyond subordination to a law without significance, a new Kafka has opened himself to us, a Kafka who provides us with insights about the structure of the law and its relation to life, a Kafka who offers a way out, a Kafka who sees possibilities to find freedom beyond subordination. This is Agamben's joyful Kafka. For there is joy in the assurance that in seemingly hopeless situations – the exposure to the violence of the state that claims to protect us from it – there is also a possibility, a messianic reversal that Kafka described so many times in his work.

The possibility emerges from the experiment that Agamben sees in literature and philosophical thought. These experiments are concerned not so much with the rightness or wrongness of hypotheses as with forms of life. Those who conduct these experiments put their own ways of being at stake (RW). And Kafka, as no other, has left us with a rich legacy of life experiments, experiments that have produced forms of life that twist the bare, sacral life that we meet in metaphysical politics, forms of life that change law, life, power, language and time.

Law

We are inclined to think of our political situation in terms of a social contract, free will and civil rights and to distinguish our democracy from sovereign power. But in Kafka's work, the law appears to be in force without significance. The sovereign has suspended the law by applying its most fundamental instrument: the state of exception. And this, according to Agamben, is how we should understand our contemporary political situation: subjected to a power that is in force but has no significance.

Kafka's work shows us that the only true response to a law that is in force without significance, a door that is open to nothing, is to go along with it, to walk the blind alley and take law to its extreme point until there is no other option left than to close the door. By acting as if he wants to enter, while knowing that there is nothing to enter, the man from the country forces the doorkeeper to finally close the door, to cancel the law's being in force while having no significance. By acting as if he does not notice the silence of the Sirens, Odysseus is victorious – not only over their singing, but also over their silence and he leaves them behind in confusion. But, as Kafka's Sancho Panza discovered, this revelation of the world as a wooden framework is not a salvation that everyone appreciates.

We should be cautious that we do not take the task of the doorkeeper on us, guarding a law that has no content and maintaining its being in force. Although Joseph K. tries to enter the law by accusing himself of his own innocence, hoping to transform the law from within, it may be better not to accept the law's invitation to enter it and to remain outside the law. With Bucephalus we may leaf through the old law books, to study it or play with it, as an object that has fallen into disuse.

Our political 'actions' in that sense would not consist of an act of a specific actor with an intention towards a goal, but of radical passivity, of gestures. Bucephalus' study is not so much an act (studying) with a purpose (restoring or fulfilling the law) but a gesture, an unending situation between undergoing and undertaking. Gestures do not have an *a priori* established meaning; rather, it is a matter of not acting in acting, of doing something while nothing seems to happen. Gestures are the pure demonstration of being-thus, as in Kafka's story on the Oklahoma theatre, where everybody's common gesturality is immediately part of the play.

Life

The origin of the structure of exception inherent to the law lies in its ambivalent position with respect to life. Law attempts to define human life as its subject, to define a 'work of man' that will bring its happiness and that is the goal of politics. But since there is not such a work, no transcendence of human being, each attempt to determine it leads to exclusion and dehumanization. Current politics attempts to find the *zoē* of the *bios* but ends up creating bare life: biological life deprived of all its humanity, a life about which life or death can be decided easily. Life that is characterized by a blurring between private and public life: politics extending itself deep into the private realm, just as in Joseph K.'s 'bedroom trial'.

Different attempts have been undertaken to revolt against this bare life: opposing it to a true human subject as bearer of human values, or claiming that all life is sacred. Agamben shows that all these attempts only echo the same metaphysical structure that created bare life in the first place. Kafka's creatures, on the contrary, twist this concept of the subject, the idea of a work of man, of the sacrality of life and the distinction between human and animal aspects of life. These creatures, like Odradek, or the strange dogs at which the researches of the dog are aimed, seem to live outside the law. Law loses its transcendence over them because they frustrate the boundaries that law tries to draw. The singing dogs and the moon dogs, these intermediate forms between animals and non-animals, seem not to respond to the laws of dogs but live in a world of freedom.

Odradek has no origin and no purpose. But although he is without purpose, in his own way he seems to be complete. And, more importantly, he cannot die: something that is without an activity of its own cannot be used up. On the one hand, Odradek is forgotten, worthless; on the other hand, he opens up a new world in which things have lost their relation to functionality and instrumentality. This is a world outside the law.

Kafka's useless assistants and messengers also show a world of irreparable being-thus, behind political distinctions. For these creatures, the unfinished and the unwieldy, there is hope. And by showing their being-thus they open a new world for us, the judges, lawyers, guards, the Count and Klamm, for everyone who is subordinated to power. The assistants represent our relation to that which has been lost, to that which needs to be saved but can remain as it is, irreparable and thus saved. The unsavable makes salvation possible, makes being-thus possible. This being-thus is no remedy, no solution, it is a redemption at the point at which we no longer want to be saved. This is the hope that is not for us.

Power

In annulling a presupposed identity, in making the boundaries inoperative between *zoē* and *bios*, act and non-act, between law and life, between immanence and transcendence, not only the subject is freed, but also sovereign power. According to Agamben, this is the new Kabbalah that Kafka is preparing. This is evident from the many limbo situations that he describes. Limbo situations, not in which God has forgotten the non-baptized children, but in which they have forgotten God from the start, situations in which the condemned man in 'In the Penal Colony' is saved without his knowing or being aware of it and who only laughs quietly to himself. Or the assault on the final earthly frontiers of the land surveyor K., which is at the same time an assault from above. Kafka's work offers not only liberation for the creatures that are subject to a higher power, but also for that power itself. The moment the power loses its subject, it also collapses into a being-thus; it loses transcendence. And what image of that is more beautiful than the officer in the penal colony who embodies both the sovereign and the Messiah?

Language

Agamben claims that the same metaphysical structure that underlies the relation between law and life also penetrates our conceptions of language and time. Just like the law's being in force without significance, language presupposes an outside, a transcendence and a subject. To come to a new understanding, we must walk the blind alley of language to the end and return to language, just like Kafka's person in suspended animation, or the impatience of literature. The return from suspended animation shows that no transcendence is possible, only a return from immanence. The person who has been in a state of suspended animation stops pretending that there is anything 'outside' it. If we apply this return to language, the word no longer exists beyond the word, just as the law's being in force beyond its significance was made inoperative.

Only by traversing language as a kind of blind alley can the non-linguistic, silenced by the word, be expressed. This can also be seen in Kafka's parable on parables, which shows that if we ourselves become language, go along with language, the difference between language and a subject outside of language disappears. True happiness can be reached only if we are freed from the Babel of names. Justice demands the revocation and destruction of language and law, as the officer in the penal colony shows when he takes the place of the condemned man and the machine of language falls apart when having to execute the unexecutable command 'be just'.

Time

A true revolution not only changes the world, but also changes time, changes our experience of time as a fleeting continuum of moments and our inability to find our place in time. According to Agamben, the task of tradition was to help us to find our place in history and that of art was to help us find our place in the present. But neither can fulfill their task any longer. Kafka offers us an inversed task of both art and tradition.

Kafka's art shows that we can make our inability to find our place in time the very ground on which we happily live. Kafka's Chinese from the south cheerfully mix up the order of dynasty which rules them, pitying the officials trapped in chronological time.

Regarding tradition, Kafka sacrifices truth for the sake of transmissibility: transmissibility raises its mighty paw against the truth. Like the students who no longer write, the horse Bucephalus who has cast off Alexander the

Great and leafs through law books and Sancho Panza who calmly follows Don Quixote, this removes the burden of accumulated traditions from our backs.

In this shift towards transmissibility, transmissibility no longer displays a transcendent truth but a being-thus: survival beyond its significance. Chronological significance is abandoned for the sake of the survival of the previous world, of the prehistoric depths. As a residue from this old time, Odradek is a small door in our chronological view of time, a *Nachleben*. But what does this new transmissibility look like? It is the transmissibility of the fact that there is nothing to transmit, as the closed fist in Babel's city coat of arms shows.

Therefore, Kafka's Messiah will come only when we have abandoned chronological time – not on the last day, which is still a chronological concept, but the day after that, the last day of all. But if we have abandoned our idea of time as a fleeting continuum of moments, we will notice that the Messiah has already come without our having noticed it and that each moment is the small door through which the Messiah can enter because he does not come after this time but exists alongside this time. We simply have to recognize this.

Finding freedom beyond subordination

Such are the strategies aiming directly at the structure of the law; strategies trying to inverse the subject of law and, with the crumbling of this subject, we saw that power itself also starts to crumble; strategies aiming at a new concept of language and time, freed from the metaphysical assumptions that linked them to politics. But how does Agamben's Kafka help us? Some doubt remains whether he has truly removed the burden from our backs and that we now know what we need to 'do'. If Agamben's critics would have it their way, he only entertained us in 'a grand and profitable way', or, worse, he urges us to resistance in the role of a Don Quixote.

In that respect Agamben's method has urged us to look for 'what can be developed' (*Entwickelungsfähigkeit*), as paradigms, as literary experiments. Agamben's Kafka is a contrast medium that helps us take a different view of politics, action and the subject. His shattered references blink up in various crucial points in his books and a thorough reading shows a great coherence in these references. And it needs to be repeated time and again: this is a cheerful message. Agamben's Kafka alerts one to possibilities of inversion of certain structures in society and politics.

But how fruitful is this approach? That is something that we will have to test in our own lives as well, looking for the diffuse moments of power, irrevocably putting our lives at stake, our concepts of language and time, until hope is no longer for us. We will be aided, at the back of our head, by Kafka's shimmering lightness and merciless humour and, when we least expect it, by his laughter.

Bibliography

Abbott, Mathew. 'The Creature before the Law: Notes on Walter Benjamin's Critique of Violence'. *Colloquy text theory critique* 16, (2008): 80–96.

Adorno, Theodor Wiesengrund. 'Notes on Kafka'. In *Prisms*. Cambridge: MIT Press, 1983.

Adorno, Theodor Wiesengrund and Ernst Bloch. 'Etwas Fehlt: Über Die Widersprüche Der Utopischen Sehnsucht'. In *Tendenz, Latenz, Utopie: Werkausgabe Ergäzungsband*, edited by Ernst Bloch, 350–68. Frankfurt: Suhrkamp, 1985.

Agamben, Giorgio. *The Coming Community, Notes on politics*. Minneapolis: University of Minnesota Press, 1993.

—*The End of the Poem: Studies in Poetics*. Stanford, CA: Stanford University Press, 1999.

—'The Eternal Return and the Paradox of Passion'. *Stanford Italian Review* 6, no. 1–2 (1986): 9–17.

—*Homo Sacer: Sovereign Power and Bare Life*. Stanford, CA: Stanford University Press, 1998.

—*Idea of Prose*. Albany: State University of New York Press, 1995.

—'Il Pozzo Di Babele'. *Tempo presente* 11, no. November (1966): 42–50.

—*Image et Mémoire. Écrits sur L'image, la Danse et le Cinéma*. Paris: Desclée de Brouwer, 2004.

—*Infancy and History: The Destruction of Experience*. London; New York: Verso, 1993.

—'K.' In *The Work of Giorgio Agamben : Law, Literature, Life*, edited by Nicholas Heron, Justin Clemens and Alex Murray, 66–81. Edinburgh: Edinburgh University Press, 2008.

—*The Kingdom and the Glory: For a Theological Genealogy of Economy and Government. Homo Sacer Ii.2*. Stanford, CA: Stanford University Press, 2011.

—*Language and Death: The Place of Negativity*. Minneapolis: University of Minnesota Press, 1991.

—*The Man without Content*. Stanford, CA: Stanford University Press, 1999.

—*Means without End: Notes on Politics*, Theory out of Bounds. Minneapolis: University of Minnesota Press, 2000.

—'The Messiah and the Sovereign: The Problem of Law in Walter Benjamin'. In *Potentialities: Collected Essays in Philosophy*, edited by W. Hamacher and D. E. Wellbery, 160–77. Stanford, CA: Stanford University Press, 1999/1992.

—*Nudities*. Stanford, CA: Stanford University Press, 2010.

—'On Tiqqun'. Available at http://anarchistwithoutcontent.wordpress.com/2010/04/18/tiqqun-apocrypha-repost, 2009. Access date: 11/06/12.

—*The Open: Man and Animal*. Stanford, CA: Stanford University Press, 2004.

—*Potentialities: Collected Essays in Philosophy*, Meridian: Crossing Aesthetics. Stanford, CA: Stanford University Press, 1999.
—*Profanations*. New York: Zone Books, 2007.
—'Quattro Glosse a Kafka'. *Rivista di estetica* 26, no. 22 (1986): 37–44.
—*Remnants of Auschwitz: The Witness and the Archive*. New York: Zone Books 1999.
—*The Sacrament of Language: An Archaeology of the Oath*. Stanford, CA: Stanford University Press, 2010.
—*The Signature of All Things: On Method*. New York: Zone Books, 2009.
—*Stanzas: Word and Phantasm in Western Culture*, Theory and History of Literature. Minneapolis: University of Minnesota Press, 1993.
—*State of Exception*. Chicago: University of Chicago Press, 2005.
—'Terrorism or Tragicomedy'. *Libération* November 19, (2008).
—'The Thing Itself'. *Contemporary Italian Thought* 16.2, no. 53 (1987): 18–28.
—'The Time That Is Left'. *Epoché* 7, no. 1 (2002): 1–14.
—*The Time That Remains: A Commentary on the Letter to the Romans*, Meridian, Crossing Aesthetics. Stanford, CA: Stanford University Press, 2005.
—'Vorwort'. In *Die Beamten Des Himmels: Über Engel*, 11–27. Frankfurt am Main/Leipzig: Verlag der Weltreligionen, 2007.
—'Warum War Und Ist Robert Walser So Wichtig?' (2005). Available at http://www.mikrogramme.de/e945/e935/index_ger.html. Access date: 11/06/12.
—'What Is a Paradigm?' Available at http://www.egs.edu/faculty/agamben/agamben-what-is-a-paradigm-2002.html (2002). Access date: 11/06/12.
—'*What Is an Apparatus?' And Other Essays*. Stanford, CA: Stanford University Press, 2009.
—'The Work of Man'. In *Giorgio Agamben: Sovereignty and Life*, edited by Matthew Calarco and Steven DeCaroli, 1–11. Stanford, CA: Stanford University Press, 2007.
Agamben, Giorgio and Judith Butler. *Eichmann, Law and Justice*. Available at http://www.egs.edu/faculty/giorgio-agamben/videos/eichmann-law-and-justice/, 2009. Access date: 11/06/12.
Allemann, Beda. 'Kafka et l'histoire'. In *L'endurance De La Pensée: Pour Saluer Jean Beaufret.*, edited by R. Char. Paris: Plon, 1968.
Alves, Marcelo. 'Diante de la Lei: O Camponês De Kafka Não É O Abandonado De Agamben'. *Novos Estudos Juridicos* 12, no. 2 (2007): 277–84.
Aristotle. *The Nicomachean Ethics*. Minneapolis: Filiquarian Publishing, 2007.
Barthes, Roland. 'Kafka's Answer'. In *Critical Essays*, 133–39. Evanston [Ill.]: Northwestern University Press, 1972.
Bartoloni, Paolo. 'The Threshold and the Topos of the Remnant – Giorgio Agamben'. *Angelaki-Journal of the Theoretical Humanities* 13, no. 1 (2008): 51–63.
Beck, Evelyn Torton. *Kafka and the Yiddish Theater. Its Impact on Its Work*. Madison, Milwaukee and London: The University of Wisconsin Press, 1971.

Benjamin, Walter. *Selected Writings*. Cambridge, Mass.: Belknap Press, 1996.
Benjamin, Walter and Theodor Adorno. *The Complete Correspondence, 1928–1940*. Cambridge: Polity Press, 1999.
Benjamin, Walter and Gershom Scholem. *The Correspondence of Walter Benjamin and Gershom Scholem, 1932–1940*. 1st Harvard University Press pbk. edn. Cambridge, MA: Harvard University Press, 1992.
Cacciari, Massimo. *Icone della Legge*. Milan: Adelphi, 1985.
Calvino, Italo. *Six Memos for the Next Millennium*. Cambridge MA: Harvard University Press, 1988.
Camus, Albert. 'Hope and the Absurd in the World of Franz Kafka'. In *Kafka: A Collection of Critical Essays*, edited by R. D. Gray. New Jersey: Prentice-Hall, 1962.
DeCauter, Lieven. 'De Bloedige Mystificaties van de Nieuwe Wereldorde'. *De witte raaf* 108, (2004): 7–9.
DelaDurantaye, Leland. 'Agamben's Potential'. *Diacritics* 30, no. 2 (2000): 3–24.
—*Giorgio Agamben: A Critical Introduction*. Stanford, CA: Stanford University Press, 2009.
Deleuze, Gilles and Félix Guattari. *Kafka. Toward a Minor Literature*. Minneapolis, London: University of Minnesota Press, 1975/1986.
—*A Thousand Plateaus: Capitalism and Schizophrenia*. London: Athlone Press, 1988.
DeNicola, Paul. 'Literature as Pure Mediality: Kafka and the Scene of Writing'. The European Graduate School, 2007.
Derrida, Jacques. 'Force of Law'. *Cardozo Law Review* 11, (1990): 919–1045
Dickinson, Colby. *Agamben and Theology*. New York: Continuum, 2011.
Dolar, Mladen. *A Voice and Nothing More*. Cambridge: MIT Press, 2006.
Grözinger, Karl-Erich. *Kafka and Kabbalah*. New York: Continuum, 1994.
Gustafsson, Håkan. '"As If": Behind before the Law'. *Law and Critique* 6, no. 1 (1996): 99–115.
Hamacher, Werner. 'The Gesture in the Name: On Benjamin and Kafka'. In *Premises: Essays on Philosophy and Literature from Kant to Celan*, 294–336. Stanford: Stanford University Press, 1999.
Hanssen, Beatrice. *Walter Benjamin's Other History: Of Stones, Animals, Human Beings and Angels*. Berkeley, CA: University of California Press, 1998.
Heller-Roazen, Daniel. 'To Read What Was Never Written'. In *Potentialities. Collected Essays in Philosophy*, edited by Daniel Heller-Roazen. Stanford, CA: Stanford University Press, 1999.
Herr, Michael. *Kubrick*. New York: Grove Press, 2001.
Hodin, Josef Paul. 'Memories of Franz Kafka'. *Horizon* 17, no. 97 (1948): 26–46.
Hurwitz, Siegmund. *Die Gestalt des Sterbenden Messias; Religionspsychologische Aspekte der Jüdischen Apokalyptik*. Zürich: Rascher Verlag, 1958.
Hutchinson, Anthony. *Shame and Philosophy: An Investigation in the Philosophy of Emotions and Ethics*. Palgrave Macmillan, 2008.

Johnson, David E. '"As If" the Time Were Now: Deconstructing Agamben'. *South Atlantic Quarterly* 106, no. 2 (2007): 265–90.
Kafka, Franz. *Amerika: The Missing Person*. Trans. M. Harman. New York: Schocken Books, 2008.
—*The Blue Octavo Notebooks*. Massachusetts: Exact Change, 1991.
—*The Castle*. Trans. M. Harman. New York: Schocken Books, 1998b.
—*The Complete Stories*. Trans. by N. N. Glatzer. New York: Schocken Books, 1995.
—*Dearest Father: Stories and Other Writings*. Trans. Ernst Kaiser and Eithne Wilkins. New York: Schocken Books, 1954.
—*The Diaries, 1910–1923*. New York: Schocken Books, 1988.
—'"He" Notes from the Year 1920'. In *The Great Wall of China. Stories and Reflections*. New York: Schocken Books, 1970b.
—*Letters to Friends, Family and Editors*. New York: Schocken Books, 1977.
—*Letters to Milena*. Trans. Philip Boehm. New York: Schocken Books, 1990.
—'Reflections on Sin, Pain, Hope and the True Way'. In *The Great Wall of China. Stories and Reflections*. New York: Schocken Books, 1970a.
—*Selected Stories*. Trans. Stanley Corngold. New York: W. W. Norton, 2007.
—*The Trial*. Trans. Breon Mitchell. New York: Schocken Books, 2009.
Kiesow, Rainer Maria. Law and Life. In *Politics, Metaphysics and Death. Essays on Giorgio Agamben's Homo Sacer*, edited by Andrew Norris, 248–62. Durham, London: Duke University Press, 2005.
Kishik, David. *The Power of Life: Agamben and the Coming Politics*. Stanford, CA: Stanford University Press, 2011.
Kraft, Werner. *Franz Kafka. Durchdringung und Geheimnis*. Frankfurt am Main: Suhrkamp, 1972.
Lebovic, Nitzan. 'The Jerusalem School: The Theopolitical Hour'. *New German Critique 105*, 35 (3): 97–120, 2008.
—'Benjamins Sumpflogik: Ein Kommentar Zur Agambens Kafka Und Benjamin Lektüre'. In *Profanes Leben: Walter Benjamins Dialektik Der Sakularisierung*, edited by Daniel Weidner, 191–212. Frankfurt am Main Suhrkamp, 2010.
Leitgeb, Hanna and Cornelia Vismann. 'Das Unheilige Leben. Ein Gespräch mit dem Italienischen Philosophen Giorgio Agamben (Interview)'. *Literaturen* 2, no. 1 (2001): 16–21.
Levi, Primo. *Survival in Auschwitz and the Reawakening: Two Memoirs*. New York: Summit Books, 1986.
Liska, Vivian. 'Als Ob Nicht. Messianismus in Giorgio Agambens Kafka-Lektüren'. In *Die Gouvernementale Maschine. Zur Politischen Philosophie Giorgio Agambens*, edited by J. Böckelmann and F. Meier, 75–90. Münster: Unrast-verlag, 2007.
—'Der Messias in Der Schriftmaschine. Gesetz Und Schrift in Giorgio Agambens Kafka-Lektüren'. *Trans. Internet-Zeitschrift für Kulturwissenschaften* 16, (2006).
—'Die Tradierbarkeit Der Lücke in Der Zeit. Arendt, Agamben und Kafka'. In *Hannah Arendt Und Giorigo Agamben. Parallelen, Perspektiven, Kontoversen,*

edited by Eva Geulen, Kai Kauffmann and Georg Mein, 191–207. München: Wilhelm Fink Verlag, 2008.

—'The Messiah before the Law. Giorgio Agamben, Walter Benjamin Und Kafka'. In *Benjamin – Agamben. Politics, Messianism, Kabbalah*, edited by Claas Morgenroth Vittoria Borso, Karl Solibakke and Bernd Witte, 159–75 Translation of: Als ob Nicht. Messianismus in Giorgio Agambens Kafka-Lektüren. Würzburg: Königshausen and Neumann, 2010.

Lüdemann, Susanne. '"*Geltung Ohne Bedeutung*" Zur Architektonik des Gesetzes bei Franz Kafka und Giorgio Agamben'. *Zeitschrift Fur Deutsche Philologie* 124, no. 4 (2005): 499–519.

Martel, James. 'The Messiah Who Comes and Goes: Franz Kafka on Redemption, Conspiracy and Community'. *Theory & Event* 12, no. 3 (2009).

McLoughlin, Daniel. 'The Politics of Caesura: Giorgio Agamben on Language and the Law'. *Law and Critique* 20, no. 2 (2009): 163–76.

Mesnard, Philippe and Claudine Kahan. *Giorgio Agamben á l'épreuve d'Auschwitz. Temoignages/Interpretations*. Paris: Éditions Kimé, 2001.

Mills, Catherine. 'Agamben's Messianic Politics. Biopolitics, Abandonment and Happy Life'. *Contretemps 5* December 2004, (2004): 42–62.

—*The Philosophy of Agamben*. Stocksfield, UK: Acumen, 2008b.

—'Playing with Law. Agamben and Derrida on Postjuridical Justice'. *The South Atlantic Quarterly* 107, no. 1. The Agamben Effect (2008a): 15–37.

Minden, Michael. 'Kafka's "Josefine Die Sängerin Oder Das Volk Der Mäuse"'. *German Life and Letter* 62, no. 3 (2009): 297–310.

Moran, Brendan. 'An Inhumanly Wise Shame'. *The European Legacy* 14, no. 5 (2009): 573–85.

—'Kafka's Prophecy, with Benjamin and Agamben'. *Philosophy Today* 55, no. Sep supplement (2011): 285–91.

Morgan, Alastair. '"A Figure of Annihilated Human Existence": Agamben and Adorno on Gesture'. *Law Critique* 2009, no. 2 (2009).

Morris, Daniel. 'Life of Something Like It. The Philosophical Chiaroscuro of Giorgio Agamben'. *Bookforum*, Summer 2004, (2004).

Murray, Alex. *Giorgio Agamben*, Routledge Critical Thinkers. London, New York: Routledge, 2009.

Murray, Alex and Jessica Whyte. *The Agamben Dictionary*. Edinburgh: Edinburgh University Press, 2011.

Nedoh, Boštjan. 'Kafka's Land Suveyor K. Agamben's Anti-Muselmann'. *Angelaki* 16.3 (2011): 149–61.

Negri, Antonio. 'The Ripe Fruit of Redemption'. Available at www.generation-online.org/t/negriagamben.htm (2004). Access date: 11/06/12.

Negri, Antonio and Cesare Casarino. 'It's a Powerful Life: A Conversation on Contemporary Philosophy'. *Cultural Critique* 57, no. Spring (2004): 151–83.

Nietzsche, Friedrich. *The Gay Science: With a Prelude in Rhymes and an Appendix of Songs*. Trans. Walter Kaufmann. New York: Vintage Books, 1974.

—*Thus Spoke Zarathustra: A Book for All and None*. Trans. Walter Kaufmann. New York: Random House, 1995.

Nolan, Kevin. 'Getting Past Odradek'. In *Contemporary Poetics*, edited by Louis Armand, 41–57. Evanston: Northwestern University Press, 2007.

Pawel, Ernst. *The Nightmare of Reason: A Life of Franz Kafka*. New York: Farrar, Straus, Giroux, 1984.

Potte-Bonneville, Mathieu and Stany Grelet. 'Une Biopolitique Mineure: Entretien avec Giorgio Agamben'. *Vacarme* 10, (1999): 4–10.

Raoul-Duval, Jacqueline. *Kafka, l'Éternel Fiancé*. Paris: Flammarion, 2011.

Rehberg, Peter. *Lachen Lesen. Zur Komik der Moderne bei Kafka*. Bielefeld: Verlag, 2007.

Robert, Marthe. *L'Ancien et le Nouveau: De Don Quichotte à Kafka*. Paris: Éditions Payot, 1967.

Salzani, Carlo. 'In a Messianic Gesture: Agamben with Kafka'. In *Issei conference 'Thought in Science and Fiction'*. Ankara, Turkey, 2–6 August, 2010a.

—'"The Sentence Is the Goal': Agamben's Notion of Law'. In *Law, Morality and Power: Global Perspectives on Violence and the State*, edited by Stephen King, Carlo Salzani and Owen Staley, 3–11. Freeland: The Inter-Disciplinary Press, 2010b.

Santner, Eric L. *On Creaturely Life: Rilke, Benjamin, Sebald*. Chicago and London: University of Chicago Press, 2006.

Snoek, Anke. 'Agamben's Foucault: An Overview'. *Foucault studies* no. 10 (2010): 44–67.

Sontag, Susan. *Against Interpretation*. London: Eyre & Spottiswoode, 1967.

Sternstein, Malynne. 'Laughter, Gesture and Flesh: Kafka's "In the Penal Colony"'. *Modernism / modernity* 8, no. 2 (2001): 315–23.

Stimilli, Davide. *Fisionomia Di Kafka*. Turino: Bollati Boringhieri 2001.

Ten Bos, René. 'On the Possibility of Formless Life: Agamben's Politics of the Gesture'. *Ephemera. theory & politics in organization* 5, no. 1 (2005): 26–44.

Udoff, Alan. 'Kafka's Question'. In *Kafka and the Contemporary Critical Performance*, edited by Alan Udoff, viii, 277. Bloomington: Indiana University Press, 1987.

Vatter, Miguel. 'In Odradek's World: Bare Life and Historical Materialism in Agamben and Benjamin'. *Diacritics* 38, no. 3 (2008): 45–70.

Wall, Thomas Carl. *Radical Passivity: Lévinas, Blanchot and Agamben*. New York: State University of New York Press, 1999.

Watkin, William. *The Literary Agamben*. New York: Continuum, 2010.

Weber, Samuel. 'Going Along for the Ride. Violence and Gesture. Agamben Reading Benjamin Reading Kafka Reading Cervantes'. *The Germanic Review* January 2006, (2006).

Whyte, Jessica. '"Its Silent Working Was a Delusion"' In *The Work of Giorgio Agamben: Law, Literature, Life*, edited by Nicholas Heron, Justin Clemens and Alex Murray, 66–81. Edinburgh: Edinburgh University Press, 2008.

Zorita, Eduardo Mauro. 'Para una Lectura Crítica de *Hacia la Crítica de la Violencia* de Walter Benjamin: Schmitt, Kafka, Agamben'. *Isegoria* no. 41 (2009): 267–76.

Index